Ambrose Chapel

www.stickingplacebooks.com

© Brian De Palma 2025
Introduction © James Kenney
Cover design by Maria Wilk

© Sticking Place Books 2025

ISBN 978-1-942782-96-4

Ambrose Chapel

Brian De Palma

Sticking Place Books
New York

Invisible Ink:
Brian De Palma's *Ambrose Chapel* and the Masterpiece That Wasn't

Brian De Palma is one of the most dazzling, divisive, and endlessly debated auteurs in world cinema—a filmmaker whose career spans over five decades and who has, at various turns, been dubbed a master of suspense, a master of style, a master of pastiche, and a master of provocation. But perhaps the title that fits him best is this: the preeminent master of being misunderstood.

Few major directors have generated such consistently visceral responses—rapturous admiration from wiser quarters, and exasperated dismissal from misguided others. His films don't simply entertain; they provoke, unsettle, implicate. And in a culture increasingly allergic to ambiguity, De Palma's slippery, labyrinthine moralities and ruthless, scrutinizing camera have often made him a target.

His body of work is formidable, and, I'd argue, unassailable. *Sisters* (1973), *Phantom of the Paradise* (1974), *Obsession* (1976), *Carrie* (1976), *The Fury* (1978), *Dressed to Kill* (1980), *Blow Out* (1981), *Scarface* (1983), *Body Double* (1984), *The Untouchables* (1987), *Casualties of War* (1989), *Raising Cane* (1992), *Carlito's Way* (1993), *Mission: Impossible* (1996), *Snake Eyes* (1998), *Mission to Mars* (2000), and *Femme Fatale* (2002) are not just milestones in expressive filmmaking—they are masterclasses in cinematic language, in the grammar of image, motion, and emotional engineering. Like a painter with a blade for a brush, De Palma composes images that wound yet seduce. His frames bleed tension. His split diopters and overhead shots don't merely dazzle, they confront and unmask. And his mise-en-scène is less "blocking" than choreography: each scene plated with the precision of haute cuisine, ingredients balanced to the millimeter, garnished with dread or desire.

Too often accused of misogyny, De Palma is, in truth, one of cinema's most complicated feminists—a director who doesn't just show violence but interrogates it, who refuses to anesthetize audiences from horror. In his most devastating works (*Carrie*, *Casualties of War*, *Blow Out*, the scorched and underexplored *Redacted*), the camera becomes a witness, not a voyeur—steadfast, unblinking, moral. Unlike directors who cut away or soften the blow, De Palma lingers, holds, traps us with the characters, forcing us to see, to feel. He does not offer safety, but empathy. In a medium where detachment is often default, De Palma dares to implicate the viewer and turn the gaze back on itself.

It is from this position—of formal brilliance, moral confrontation, and perennial misreading—that *Ambrose Chapel* emerges. And yet, this unproduced screenplay from the mid-1990s feels like a strange child of that lineage: laced with a certain menacing whimsy, *Ambrose Chapel* is De Palma pivoting toward genre inversion with reflexive glee.

Chapel is a revelation, an unproduced, richly imagined screenplay that plays like a screwball thriller built atop the ruins of Cold War paranoia, Hitchcockian homage, and the director's lifelong obsessions with voyeurism, manipulation, and cinematic sleight of hand. It's a cathedral of misdirection, simultaneously light on its feet and heavy with implication, where psychological trauma pirouettes into dark comedy, and deception becomes both theme and structure.

That such a film remains unmade is itself a twist worthy of De Palma: a secret masterwork hidden in plain sight, offering its most thrilling surprises not in projection, but on the page.

Reading *Ambrose Chapel* is like hearing an unreleased movement from a familiar symphony, echoing earlier motifs but arranged in an entirely unexpected key. Its often comic tone and playful sparring between the leads mark a startling departure from the brooding gravitas of *Casualties of War* and the melancholic paranoia of *Blow Out*, yet its deeper structures—themes of surveillance, father/daughter trauma, and doubles within doubles—are unmistakably

De Palma. And it is precisely this lightness, this tonal pivot from requiem to scherzo, that makes *Ambrose Chapel* so intriguing. It emerges not from a place of triumph but from the ashes of disillusionment, following the one-two sting of *Casualties of War*—a masterpiece met with indifference—and *The Bonfire of the Vanities* (1990), a high-wire studio effort that never found balance. From that silence, De Palma didn't retreat—he recalibrated. And when he returned, it was with a new movement: not louder, but quicker, trickier, more playful.

The Ethics of Witnessing: Empathy and the Unflinching Eye

Across his body of work, Brian De Palma has been accused of lurid observation, excess, even sadism. What too often goes unrecognized is the profound moral architecture underpinning his most emotionally resonant films. He is not merely a stylist; he is a concerned witness. In *Casualties of War*, this role is explicit: the camera refuses to look away, even when every instinct tells us to blink.

Michael J. Fox's protagonist becomes the director's surrogate, a powerless bystander to a rape and murder whose anguished gaze becomes the film's ethical stance. *Casualties* insists on the victim's humanity—not as metaphor or device, but as the film's center of gravity. Its many long, uninterrupted takes deny the audience the comfort of directorial guidance, making the absence of overt manipulation feel like an unbearable, heightened presence. Ennio Morricone's aching score doesn't glorify; it grieves. When the young victim is marched across a bridge, the camera doesn't cut to action or reaction. It lingers: time stretches into mourning.

But this ethic of compassionate witnessing is not limited to *Casualties*. In *Carrie*, De Palma composes scenes of cruelty and isolation with painterly precision, only to detonate them with emotional vengeance. The blood is real, the humiliation unforgettable, but the camera is never indifferent. It suffers along with Carrie. *Blow Out*, perhaps his most politically despairing film, offers a film sound man (John Travolta) who uncovers a murder through technology, only to realize that his efforts to expose the truth are powerless against a system that feeds on spectacle. The final, desperate scream of a beloved but doomed character—recycled by a lost Travolta as a movie sound effect—is not a punchline but a tragedy: bearing witness is not always enough. In *Carlito's Way*, De Palma's gaze follows a man trying to escape his past, but his world will not allow it. It is a film steeped in regret, narrated with the clarity of someone who begins the film witnessing his own death, knowing before the story unfolds that he cannot escape unscathed the celluloid frame in which he temporarily survives to relive past mistakes.

And in *The Black Dahlia* (2006), that frame becomes a trap. In the film's most haunting sequence, a screen test of aspiring actress Elizabeth Short (Mia Kirshner) plays out as a slow, cynical seduction—by both the offscreen director and the complicit audience. We are partners in her exploitation, eyeing her with curiosity, then sensuality, then discomfort, as the audition becomes less about performance than power. When she is introduced through disquieting scenes of her screen tests, the horror is sharpened—not just by the violence we already know will befall her, but by our own role in the chain of spectatorship that renders her vulnerability all the more tragic. She is the film's center, its mutilated murder victim, and the horror is doubled, not only by the violence done to her body, but by our uneasy complicity in watching her emotional unmooring through the gaze of her exploiter.

De Palma reckons with that ethical stance further in *Body Double*, *Mission: Impossible*, and *Domino* (2019). These are also films obsessed with complicity, with characters who witness but don't act—or act too late, as hesitation proves fatal pause, leaving trusted companions and vulnerable strangers dead, the guilt lingering like an unresolved chord. These films don't just question whether seeing is believing; they explore the deeper, more unsettling guilt that arises from bearing witness while being unable to intervene, a condition that, of course, mirrors the audience's own position. As spectators, we are always watching from the sidelines, implicated yet powerless, which is precisely why De Palma's work is so disquieting, as we're repeatedly moved to act in his films, but, of course, we never can. The camera draws us in, implicating us. We enjoy the view. We crave the reveal. And then we're left to confront the unsettling truth we've absorbed. De Palma's greatest trick may be that he turns the tools of spectacle against themselves, a subversive impulse that, despite his success with big-budget action spectacles like *The Fury*, *Scarface*, *The Untouchables*, and *Mission: Impossible*, kept him from ever being fully embraced by the industry as a reliable architect of mainstream blockbusters. His signature flourishes—split diopters, split screens, slow motion, baroque compositions—never anesthetize violence; they magnify its trauma. His camera doesn't shield us from horror; it locks us inside it. Can De Palma's use of such cinematic devices at times be perceived as acts of sadism? From one angle, yes—they can feel punishing, even cruel, in their refusal to let us look away. But that discomfort is the point. The ultimate ambition is disquietingly moral: to make us feel, not escape. To confront violence not as abstraction, but as emotional fact.

In a medium built on illusion, De Palma wields tremendous style to pierce through to deeper truths, evoking genuine emotions and psychological intensity that few filmmakers dare to reach. His frames are as composed as masterful oil paintings, but they cut like broken glass. His mise-en-scène is crafted with the precision of a visionary architect courting chaos: meticulously structured, intricate, and deliberately disorienting. This may be why *Casualties of War* and *Blow Out*, for all their craft and clarity, were met with discomfort. They may prove too effective, too honest. They offer no opportunity for relaxed detachment. Like so much of De Palma's best work, they hold up the mirror too close to the audience's face and refuse to flinch. The final image of *Casualties*—a ghostly echo of a girl who cannot be saved—offers no release, only resonance. A masterpiece, yes, but one that ends its movement on a note of unresolved dissonance.

Raising Cain and the Pivot Back to Play

After the box-office collapse of *Casualties* and the infamous implosion of *Bonfire*, De Palma found himself at a crossroads. The master composer had lost his orchestra; his control was diluted by studio interference; his intentions misread. But instead of chasing safe hits or retreating into silence, De Palma turned inward, toward the very techniques and tonalities that first defined his voice.

The result was *Raising Cain* (1992), a lower-budget thriller that plays like a fragmented fugue, brash, unrestrained, and gleefully self-referential. It is a De Palma film about De Palma films: doubles within doubles, unreliable perspectives, and a flamboyant father figure splitting his child's psyche in two. In *Cain*, the camera moves not with solemnity but with swagger; the bravura technique and dream logic return not to moral reckoning but to psychological mischief.

It was here, in this more agile, trickster register, that De Palma began composing anew. And from that rediscovered sense of play came *Ambrose Chapel*, a script that channels the delirium of *Raising Cain* and foreshadows the doubling games of *Femme Fatale*, yet delivers them with a wink reminiscent of De Palma's early subversive comedies, *Greetings* (1968) and *Hi, Mom!* (1970), rather than with a wound.

The Trickster's Return in *Ambrose Chapel*

From its opening scenes—an apparent tale of CIA operations unfolding in the Middle East—*Ambrose Chapel* adopts the sleek posture of a geopolitical thriller, all international intrigue and stealthy rescues. But before we've even found our footing, the games are underway. The surface moves like an action film, yet the ground beneath is constantly shifting. Narrative certainties dissolve, and perception itself becomes the game. De Palma initially wraps his signature paranoia in the garb of an international spy film, but the stitches are false, the seams intentionally frayed. Beneath the genre facade, the machinery of misdirection is already in motion. The suspense is real, but so is the sleight of hand, setting the stage for a film that never stops rearranging its own narrative furniture.

A monstrous father figure again emerges, a broker of shadow-state intrigue and a manipulator of his own child's psyche, replaying a familiar chord from *Raising Cain*, *Sisters*, and *Mission: Impossible*. But here, the controlling patriarch becomes almost farcical, a puppet master whose strings are as tangled as the narrative itself. The plot is intricate but elegantly paced, its web of surveillance, shifting loyalties, and misread intentions drawn so tight that even the antagonists are left scrambling to understand the bigger picture. That pervasive uncertainty isn't a flaw; it's part of the film's sly appeal. In *Ambrose Chapel*, no one—not even the bad guys—has a firm grip on the truth, and that sustained disorientation becomes a source of both suspense and dark amusement.

What's new is the rhythm. The screenplay's leads, an earnest psychiatrist and put-upon newscaster, don't just navigate the maze—they dance through it. Dialogue crackles, gags land mid-chaos (watch out for that figurine collection!), and danger is met not with dread, but delight. *Ambrose Chapel* is a screwball thriller in darker clothing—ultimately, a romantic comedy stitched together from the paranoia and cinematic trickery of De Palma's earlier psychological thrillers such as *Dressed to Kill* and *Blow Out* and action films like *Mission: Impossible* and *The Fury*.

The set pieces are pure De Palma, but their effect has shifted. A sequence involving a misused TV remote triggering a street-level slaughter of rapists by our heroine escalates into a revenge fantasia that feels like Abel Ferrara's *Ms. 45* (1981) restaged by Jacques Tati. Crosscutting, which in *Casualties of War*, *Dressed to Kill*, and *Blow Out* lengthens suffering into opera, here becomes comic ballet: precision timing deployed to mischievous ends. A slow-motion flourish might delay a trauma in *Chapel*, but might also set up a good-humored punchline.

And through it all, De Palma winks, acknowledging his influences even as he outpaces them. Hitchcock isn't just referenced but audaciously repurposed, with *The Man Who*

Knew Too Much (1956) serving as a structural keystone, its concert-hall climax reimagined as both homage and metafictional game. One of the script's wryest nods is its gaggle of bleach-blonde Mexican ladies standing in for Hitchcock's archetypal icy blondes, a sly visual pun that collapses reverence into satire. It's both parody and tribute: De Palma acknowledging the master while rewriting the performance, conducting from within the score even as he scrambles its time signature.

The DNA of *Ambrose Chapel* is deeply De Palma, but the tone is surprisingly giddy, even liberatory. *Raising Cain* had rekindled this playfulness, largely dormant for nearly a decade, while *Ambrose Chapel* lets De Palma's wildest, most unrestrained impulses run riot. This is a filmmaker rediscovering pleasure, not only in narrative construction, but in the possibilities of visual storytelling embedded in the screenplay. It revels in crosscutting sequences, image-driven narrative—the collection of destroyed figurines, a sky full of colorful balloons—and moments that invite full-blown operatic excess, including detailed, complex, climactic staging of an actual opera, *Tosca*. And this visual exuberance is in service of material that grows lighter, not darker, as it unfolds. Rather than culminating in violence or despair, *Ambrose Chapel* builds toward confusion, absurdity, and a kind of comic release—a rare tonal inversion in De Palma's body of work, and a tantalizing glimpse of a master playing against his own shadow.

A New Grace Note

For all its playfulness, the screenplay also carries an unexpected, eccentric tenderness. De Palma, so often accused of pure cynicism, subjects his heroine to considerable hardship, yet gradually adopts a more protective and empathetic stance toward her. Unlike *Carrie*, *Dressed to Kill*, or *The Fury*, which end in rupture and rage, *Ambrose Chapel* arcs toward grace. The woman, manipulated by men both good and bad throughout the film with a metaphoric "kiss," asserts her authority with a literal kiss as the film fades to black.

It anticipates the tonal evolution that blooms fully in the later *Femme Fatale*, *Mission to Mars*, and *Snake Eyes*, where

De Palma's lush, calculating style coexists with a flicker of romanticism in uneasy but compelling harmony. That same harmonic friction—between menace and exuberance, paranoia and play—finds its imagined mirror in the screenplay's vibrant setting. Mexico City, as envisioned in *Ambrose Chapel*, broods with surveillance and danger, yet pulses with energy and sensual unpredictability. We can only theorize how De Palma might have rendered it onscreen, but the script suggests a city he would have painted like a baroque master—ornate, theatrical, and full of shadowed depths. Not documentary realism, but chiaroscuro myth. Mexico City is "a place that has always fascinated me," he notes in his brief discussion of *Chapel* in *De Palma on De Palma*, his book-length conversation with Laurent Bouzereau and Samuel Blumenfeld (Sticking Place Books, 2024), and here it becomes not just a backdrop but a collaborator in the film's expressive architecture—a labyrinthine stage for misdirection, revelation, and reversal.

The Score Unplayed

Ultimately, *Ambrose Chapel* is not just a revelatory, thrilling screenplay; it is a vital hinge in De Palma's artistic development. It reframes his familiar themes—doubling, surveillance, manipulation—not as traps, but as tools for his heroine's ultimate liberation. Though never filmed, it now can be read, studied, and imagined. De Palma is a master of visual form, and while the thrilling, audacious ways he might have staged *Chapel*'s baroque twists—its virtual reality recreations and outré set pieces—remain beyond our reach, we are, in a sense, granted something rarer: a glimpse of his vision unimpeded, untouched by studio interference, ratings boards, budgetary constraints, and difficult or miscast actors.

Speculation about the potential cast of *Ambrose Chapel* (had it gone into production) should intrigue De Palma scholars and cinephiles alike, particularly because the project has remained largely unknown to the public for decades. A 1998 installment of *TV Questions and Answers* revealed that the screenplay was still in circulation at that time, mentioning Téa Leoni, Brad Pitt, and Liam Neeson as potential cast members—presumably in the roles of Christe, Wolfe, and Montana, respectively (Cavasos). Additional unconfirmed reports suggest Madonna may have been considered for the role of Christe at some point, while Martin Sheen was rumored for Montana or, more intriguingly, the cryptic figure of Prince Charming. These speculative casting notes, fragmentary though they are, offer tantalizing glimpses into the film that might have been. One of the unique pleasures of reading *Ambrose Chapel* as an unproduced script is that it invites imaginative reconstruction: readers can cast the film themselves, reinventing it again and again with different actors, interpretations, and emotional tones.

Chapel is a missing movement between *Raising Cain* and *Femme Fatale*, a romantic thriller laced with comic energy, but cloaked in the mask of espionage and threaded through the psychological shadows of *Dressed to Kill*, *Blow Out*, *Sisters* and the unjustly critically marginalized *Passion* (2012) with its themes of doubling and manipulation. *Chapel*'s humor is rarely foregrounded, it glimmers at oblique angles, slipping in under cover, buried beneath conspiracies, surveillance, and fractured psyches. And yet beneath its tonal playfulness lies a striking political provocation: in 1994, De Palma imagined a villain who, unable to win an election fairly, conspires with shadowy elites and advanced technology—here, virtual reality—to manipulate the democratic process, while proposing to build a wall along the Mexican border. While the character may have then drawn inspiration from Texas industrialist Ross Perot's 1992 presidential campaign, the script's eerie 1994 premonition of Donald Trump underscores how acutely De Palma understood the theatrical nature of American politics—and how fully he anticipated its darkest turns.

With *Chapel*, De Palma doesn't abandon control; he reorients it, pulling the strings with joy instead of dread. If *Casualties of War* was a requiem—mournful, solemn, morally unyielding— then *Ambrose Chapel*, now unveiled, is his scherzo: spry, subversive, and laced with grace notes. The tempo has shifted, but the maestro remains—still conducting sensation, still orchestrating surprise, and still insisting that we listen closely.

James Kenney

TITLE: BEIRUT, 1992.

DISSOLVE TO

EXT. DEMOLISHED HOSPITAL – DAY.

CHRISTE RIVERA, a late-twenties TV news foreign correspondent, brunette, stands in the rubble of a bombed-out building.

She holds a mike and speaks directly into the camera.

> CHRISTE
> I'm reporting from the bombed-out site of the National Children's Hospital. As you can see, there's little left of the building. Standing next to me is Mr. Ali Abu of the Organization of the Oppressed on Earth. This is the group that still holds the six Americans hostages.
> (*turning to Ali Abu*)
> Were there any hostages in this building?

> ALI ABU
> No. Only innocent children. Look what your new President has done!

> CHRISTE
> But according to US intelligence, you were using American hostages as "human shields" to protect this missile factory.

> ALI ABU
> No missiles – just babies killed by your President.

> CHRISTE
> So you deny that this was a secret missile manufacturing installation?

ALI ABU
(*pulling a 9mm pistol on her*)
You come with me!

CHRISTE
I'm sorry. I don't think I understand.

ALI ABU
(*waving the gun in her face*)
MOVE!

CHRISTE
BUT YOU JUST CAN'T!

ALI ABU knocks the mike out of CHRISTE's hand and grabs her roughly by the arm.

CHRISTE
(*trying to pull away*)
LET GO OF ME!

ABU smashes CHRISTE across the face with his pistol.

The shot (a stand up) that we have been watching closes in on her as she falls.

ALI ABU turns his gun on the camera.

ALI ABU
Stay where you are! I will shoot!

The CAMERAMAN backs off and the shot widens.

Two other ARAB GUNMEN, brandishing machine guns, come into the frame and surround the defenseless CHRISTE. They pull her to her feet and drag her off to a waiting green Mercedes.

Shoving her inside, all the KIDNAPPERS pile in the car and speed off.

CUT TO

INT. TV STUDIO INTERNATIONAL NEWS DESK – NIGHT.

A grey-haired ANCHOR reads the news.

>ANCHOR
>(*looking directly into camera*)
>These scenes of the dramatic kidnapping of Christe Rivera were taken six months ago. Today we received this videotape from the Organization of the Oppressed on Earth, made by our abducted correspondent, Christe Rivera.

CUT TO

TIGHT CLOSE-UP OF THE BRUISED AND BATTERED FACE OF CHRISTE RIVERA.

Her eyes are glassy and dull.

She speaks in a painfully slow monotone.

>CHRISTE
>Over the past months I have come to understand the hopeless plight of the Shiite people. We, of the United States news media, have falsely misinformed the world. They are not hostile aggressors but simple, peace-loving people, who want nothing but harmonious co-existence. Their most powerful and honorable leader, Ali Abu, has repeatedly extended the olive branch of peace only to have

> it shot down by Criminal America and
> its Zionist Puppet. This must stop! You,
> Mr. President, must shed no more Arabic
> babies' blood! Or you, Mr. President, will
> suffer the consequences.

CHRISTE stops talking, as if she is a tape machine that is abruptly shut off.

> PULL BACK

Frozen frame of CHRISTE's broken face behind the grey-haired ANCHOR.

> ANCHOR
> The White House said today that all
> options were under consideration to obtain
> the release of Christe Rivera and the other
> hostages. When asked if the President had
> any type of direct military intervention in
> mind, there was no comment.

EXT. A BACK STREET IN BEIRUT – NIGHT.

A beaten-up VAN is parked on a deserted city street.

Twenty yards in front of the van, intersecting the street, is a narrow alley.

Five yards down the alley, recessed in the center of the road, is a metal manhole cover.

> CUT TO

INT. VAN – NIGHT.

Code name PRINCE CHARMING sits in the driver seat. He's a big, muscular man in his late forties. He speaks with a distinctive southern accent.

Next to him is a younger man, BROOKS. In the back seat are THREE OTHER MEN. They are all dressed in dark clothes and carry automatic weapons.

PRINCE CHARMING is giving them their final instructions.

> PRINCE CHARMING
> I'm going to take off in five minutes. I want you guys to follow in five. That means Kelly, Parsons, and O'Dell should be blowing the door at twenty-three hundred. I'm going to be taking the girl out the back.
> (*pointing to the manhole cover in the middle of the alley*)
> They'll come out first, and should be easy targets. Brooks and Terri, you be waiting for her there. If you do anything stupid, I'm going to have to shoot you. Remember, I'm one of them. Any questions?

The men shake their heads no.

PRINCE CHARMING takes an envelope from his pocket and gives it to BROOKS.

> PRINCE CHARMING
> If I don't get killed, make sure the Jay Bird gets this. If I don't make it, destroy it.

> BROOKS
> Yes sir.

> PRINCE CHARMING
> (*checks his watch*)
> Let's go.

EXT. VAN – NIGHT.

The driver's side door opens, and PRINCE CHARMING steps out. He quickly crosses over to the opposite side of the street.

Behind him, the rest of the COMMANDO SQUAD piles out of the van. BROOKS and TERRI move up toward the alley.

The other THREE MEN duck out of sight.

Crossing the alley and continuing halfway down the block, PRINCE CHARMING comes to a stop in front of a nondescript two-story structure.

He looks around. The street is empty.

He knocks on the door: three fast, then two slow.

A panel slides open. Through the slot, a pair of dark eyes study him for a moment.

Then the door swings open. PRINCE CHARMING goes inside.

INT. HOSTAGE HIDEOUT – NIGHT.

PRINCE CHARMING enters. ALI ABU closes the door behind him.

>   PRINCE CHARMING
> We got to move her. Quick.

>   ALI ABU
> What's wrong?

PRINCE CHARMING
In about five minutes, a United States
commando squad is going to be blasting
open that door.

ALI ABU
How did they find us?

PRINCE CHARMING
Who knows? Somebody gave you up.
What difference does it make?

Five other YOUNG ARABS, packing machine guns, drift
into the front room.

ALI ABU
I want to know who's betrayed me!

PRINCE CHARMING
Look, that's the best information I've
got. If you want me to find out where the
leak is, it will take a lot of time, and more
money than you've got.

ALI ABU
Maybe it takes no time. Maybe it's you.

PRINCE CHARMING
Me? Don't be stupid. You pay me a lot
better than the CIA. Look, I know you
don't trust me. I know you don't even
like me. But I know one thing.

ALI ABU
What do you know?

                    PRINCE CHARMING
          You need me.
                    (*looking at his watch*)
          And in two minutes you're going to
          know how much.

PRINCE CHARMING brushes past ABU and his ARMED GOONS and goes up the stairs to the second floor.

INT. SECOND FLOOR – NIGHT.

At the end of a short corridor, PRINCE CHARMING stops in front of a locked door.

Using his own key, he opens it and goes inside.

INT. HOSTAGE ROOM – NIGHT.

Against one wall is a cot, where CHRISTE lies, asleep. She wears a grey workout suit and looks surprisingly strong and healthy for a hostage.

In the middle of the room is a treadmill.

On a table next to the treadmill is a headset. A thick cord of wires is plugged into the back. They snake over to a computer resting on the floor.

Against the far wall is a workout mat, weights, a punching bag, and a trampoline.

PRINCE CHARMING crosses the room and rouses CHRISTE. She seems sedated, and he has difficulty getting the groggy girl to her feet.

                    PRINCE CHARMING
             (*speaking to her in a soft, fatherly way*)
          C'mon baby. You can make it.

INT. SECOND FLOOR – NIGHT.

PRINCE CHARMING walks CHRISTE down the corridor to the staircase.

INT. DOWNSTAIRS ROOM – NIGHT.

PRINCE CHARMING helps CHRISTE down the stairs. When he turns around he's confronted by a grim-faced ABU, backed by FIVE ARMED GOONS.

> ALI ABU
> Why didn't we keep her with the other hostages? And why so long?

> PRINCE CHARMING
> Brainwashing her. Remember? That's what you wanted, right? She gave a very moving speech. Just the way you wrote it.

> ALI ABU
> What did you need all that equipment for? Where did you get it?

> PRINCE CHARMING
> What do you care? It got the job done.

> ALI ABU
> I want answers! Why is it only you that has a key to her room?

> PRINCE CHARMING
> (*suddenly mad*)
> Because I was sick of your goons sneaking in there and fucking with her!

                    ALI ABU
               (*turning philosophical*)
     They're just bored and restless boys, they
     need a release.
               (*with sudden anger*)
     You took the key because you wanted her
     for yourself! Isn't that so?

               PRINCE CHARMING
          (*casually looking at his watch,
        which reads seven seconds before eleven*)
     Could we talk about this later? We've got
     to get out of here.

                    ALI ABU
               (*cocking his gun*)
     We talk about it NOW!

On the word "NOW" all hell breaks loose.

The door explodes.

PRINCE CHARMING knocks CHRISTE to the ground, covering her with his body.

Shattered wood and plaster spray across the room.

The TWO GOONS closest to the door are blown down.

The other TWO start firing at the smoke-filled doorway.

Their fire is immediately returned from the street.

PRINCE CHARMING grabs hold of CHRISTE and drags her out of the room.

INT. KITCHEN – NIGHT.

PRINCE CHARMING, carrying CHRISTE, enters the kitchen. He puts her gently down on the floor.

He shoves the kitchen table aside and pulls up the rug underneath.

There's a trap door in the floor. He yanks it open.

He picks up CHRISTE and carefully lowers her down inside. When she's safely resting on the floor of the tunnel, he jumps through the opening and lands in the tunnel beside her.

INT. TUNNEL – NIGHT.

PRINCE CHARMING picks CHRISTE up, throws her over his shoulder, and carries her down the tunnel. It's illuminated by a string of Christmas tree lights that stretch some thirty yards in front of them ending where the dirt tunnel cuts into a much larger sewer tunnel.

PRINCE CHARMING moves quickly through it and into the sewer.

Directly in front of him is a ladder. He slips CHRISTE off his shoulders and rests her against it.

> PRINCE CHARMING
> Can you hold on to this?

CHRISTE weakly grasps the ladder.

There's a series of short machine gun bursts from the kitchen end of the dirt tunnel.

PRINCE CHARMING looks back to see ABU and one of his men running toward him. They stumble through the dirt tunnel onto the floor of the sewer. ABU pulls himself to his feet.

                    ALI ABU
          They're all dead.

                PRINCE CHARMING
          C'mon. Get up the ladder.

ALI ABU shoves the OTHER GUNMAN up the ladder.

The GUNMAN climbs to the top, pushes open the cover, and looks around the alley.

A blast of gunfire. His head is blown off.

The gunman's body falls off the ladder onto ABU, knocking him to the hard floor of the sewer.

They both lie in a bloody heap on the ground, motionless.

PRINCE CHARMING throws CHRISTE over his shoulder and climbs up the ladder.

He stops inches below the opening to the street and calls out.

                PRINCE CHARMING
          BROOKS! IT'S ALL CLEAR.

The sound of running feet.

BROOKS' head appears over the opening.

                    BROOKS
          Yes sir.

> PRINCE CHARMING
> Take her.

BROOKS reaches down and pulls CHRISTE out of the tunnel.

> PRINCE CHARMING
> Take care of my baby.

> BROOKS
> Yes sir.

BROOKS, now holding CHRISTE in his arms, turns to leave.

> PRINCE CHARMING
> And Brooks.

> BROOKS
> (*turning back*)
> Yes sir?

> PRINCE CHARMING
> Shoot me.

> BROOKS
> Sir?

> PRINCE CHARMING
> I said shoot me! When Abu wakes up he's not going to believe you took her from me unless I'm shot.

> BROOKS
> (*nervous, his training never prepared him for this*)
> Yes, sir.

BROOKS reluctantly points his gun at PRINCE CHARMING's head.

                    PRINCE CHARMING
            I said shoot me. Not kill me.

                         BROOKS
                (*now completely unnerved*)
            Yes sir.

                    PRINCE CHARMING
            The shoulder will be just fine.

BROOKS raises his gun and points it at PRINCE CHARMING's left shoulder.

We zoom into the barrel of the gun.

It explodes.

                                            CUT TO

PRINCE CHARMING's envelope (the one he gave BROOKS earlier).

It is being sliced open with a solid gold letter opener.

Engraved on the opener is the name: JAY JEFFERSON KEEN.

We're over KEEN's shoulder, so we can't see his face. But KEEN's body is lean. His head bald.

KEEN pulls a white piece of paper out of the gutted envelope.

It has writing on it.

He flattens it out before him and starts reading.

CUT TO

Close shot on letter.

We hear PRINCE CHARMING's voice reading the letter.

> PRINCE CHARMING
> *Sleeping Beauty has been put to sleep.*
> *She has a password. She's useless without*
> *it. Looking forward to hearing from you*
> *around election time. P.S.: She's pregnant.*

FADE TO BLACK

FADE INTO

TITLE: MEXICO CITY – THE SUMMER OF 2000.

CUT TO

INT. CHRISTE'S BEDROOM – NIGHT.

CHRISTE lies in bed sleeping.

The door opens. CHRISTE's mother, MARCELA, enters the dark room. She's carrying a cup of hot coffee. She walks over and places the cup on the table next to her daughter's bed.

She gently shakes CHRISTE'S shoulder.

> MARCELA
> Honey, it's four.

CHRISTE's eyes slowly open. Now a striking blonde, in her early thirties, she sees her MOTHER and smiles up at her.

> CHRISTE
> Thanks, Mom.

INT. CHILD'S BEDROOM – NIGHT.

CHRISTE enters the room dressed in a bright red, low-cut, two-piece business suit. She's drying her hair with a bath towel.

Sleeping in a small bed is her three-year-old son, RUBEN. He lies on his back with the comforter pushed to the foot of the bed.

CHRISTE crosses the room and pulls the comforter over him. She kisses Ruben lightly on the forehead, then quietly leaves.

INT. KITCHEN – NIGHT.

CHRISTE enters. Her mother MARCELA has laid out some fresh fruit, milk, and cold cereal on the kitchen table.

CHRISTE hands her mother the towel and takes a banana from the table.

                    CHRISTE
              This will be fine.

                    MARCELA
       Won't you have a little cereal?

                    CHRISTE
            (*looking at her watch*)
              I don't have time.

MARCELA sits down at the table and pours the milk into the cereal bowl.

                    MARCELA
     Will you promise me something?

CHRISTE
What?

MARCELA
Will you talk to your boss today?

CHRISTE
(*they've had this conversation
a million times*)
Yes. Yes.
(*changing the subject*)
I'll see you at the park at nine.

MARCELA
Okay.

MARCELA picks up a spoon and starts to eat her cereal. CHRISTE kisses her goodbye, picks up her handbag, and goes out the door.

EXT. MEXICO CITY STREET – JUST BEFORE DAWN.

A lone cab, with CHRISTE inside, moves down the deserted city street.

INT. MAKE-UP ROOM AT TF1 – DAWN.

CHRISTE sits in a makeup chair as TWO MIDDLE-AGED MAKEUP AND HAIR LADIES work on her sleepy face. The MAKEUP LADY holds up a bright red eye pencil. CHRISTE brushes it away.

CHRISTE
No, no.

MAKEUP LADY
What's the matter with you?

                    CHRISTE
I don't like that color.

                    MAKEUP LADY
It's perfect. It matches your dress.

                    CHRISTE
            (*picking up a mirror and a
               brown pencil*)
This will be fine.

                    MAKEUP LADY
That ugly brown again?

                    CHRISTE
            (*dabbing the brown pencil
               on her eye lids*)
I'm supposed to look like a reporter. Not a whore.

                    HAIR LADY
            (*jamming a curler into her hair*)
Really!

                    MAKEUP LADY
Maybe if you let me make you up right, you'll get off this shift.

                    CHRISTE
You mean only the dogs go on at six in the morning?

                    MAKEUP LADY
You're not a dog, my dear. You just make yourself look like a dog.

INT. TELEVISION NEWS DESK – EARLY MORNING.

CHRISTE is on the air reading the 6 o'clock news. She speaks in Spanish. English subtitles translate her report.

                    CHRISTE
                  (*in Spanish*)
It was announced today by Press
Secretary Clement that President Cartier
and the President of the United States
will sign the revised common market
accords here in Mexico City at the end
of the week. Julio Bassene, director
of the Mexico City Opera, extended
an invitation to both presidents to his
production of Puccini's *Tosca*. Mr.
Clement said he didn't know, at this time,
if the President's busy schedule would
permit.

                                                CUT TO

INT. RECEPTION AREA OF LUIS RAMON'S OFFICE
– DAY.

CHRISTE sits on a chair across from a reception desk.

Behind it, RAMON'S BORED SECRETARY files her nails.

The door to RAMON'S OFFICE swings open and a tall, leggy, blonde bombshell walks out. This is LUCIA VILLA, the latest rising star at the station.

LUCIA walks over to CHRISTE and sits down next to her.

                    VILLA
          Whose making you up?

                    CHRISTE
          What's wrong?

                    VILLA
          That horrible brown shit on your eyes.

CHRISTE

I did it.

VILLA

Christe, would you listen to a little advice from the resident bimbo?

CHRISTE
(*smiling*)

Okay.

VILLA

The macho assholes around here think all girls on television are servants, *gatos*, whores. The more we live up to their expectations, the better the job we get.

CHRISTE

I know, Lucia. Believe me, I know.

VILLA

Christe, you're a real reporter. You've worked all over the world. That stuff you did in the Middle East was unbelievable.

CHRISTE

That's all ancient history.

VILLA

I understand. But if you're going to join the TV swimsuit competition around here, don't walk down the runway in a flour sack.
(*looking at the bags under her eyes*)
Boy, do you look tired. How long have you been on the graveyard shift?

CHRISTE

Two years.

VILLA
When was the last time you had a date?

CHRISTE
Who remembers?

VILLA
You got something against men?

CHRISTE
I like men all right. I'm just too tired to get very interested.

VILLA
Well, get interested! Men will do anything for you as long as they think they can fuck you. It's like the dog races. You got to always keep the rabbit just a little ahead of the pack. Too close? It gets ripped apart. Too far? And the dogs stop running.

CHRISTE
(*yawning*)
All this bunny wants to do is lie down and sleep.

VILLA
Is that what you're going to talk to Ramon about?

CHRISTE
Yeah. Giving me a day off.

VILLA opens the two top buttons of CHRISTE'S RED JACKET.

                    VILLA
          Lean over as much as possible, and when
          he asks you if you'd like to taste his
          money, say yes.

INT. RAMON'S OFFICE – DAY.

CHRISTE sits across from her boss, LOUIE RAMON, a hefty man in his late forties.

He stares at CHRISTE with increasing irritation. She's re-buttoned her jacket.

                    RAMON
          But I've offered you other time slots.

                    CHRISTE
          I know.

                    RAMON
          You didn't seem interested.

                    CHRISTE
               (*smiling*)
          I was interested. It just seemed that there
          was more to it than that.

                    RAMON
          What's that supposed to mean?

                    CHRISTE
          I think you know what I'm talking about.

                    RAMON
          I have no idea what you're talking about.

                    CHRISTE
          I guess that means I don't get Saturday
          off.

RAMON
Mrs. Rivera, I don't quite understand you. When you first came to work here, you refused to take any hard news assignments. I might remind you that we hired you specifically for your experience in this area.

CHRISTE
I don't know why you keep calling me Mrs. Rivera today, Louie, Christe used to be just fine. And I don't do hard news anymore. I told you that when I took this job. I am perfectly happy to read news like the rest of the starlets around here. I am just asking for a little break in the hours.

RAMON
Then I think you should be a little more accommodating.

CHRISTE
What did you have in mind?

RAMON
Julio Bassene.

CHRISTE
Give me a break, Luis. The guy's a pig. Send Rebecca. She'll be able to handle him.

RAMON
He doesn't want Rebecca. He wants you.

CHRISTE
The only reason he wants me is that he hasn't had me yet.

                    RAMON
Work it out! Then, perhaps, we'll discuss a
different schedule. Goodbye, Mrs. Rivera.

EXT. MEXICO CITY PARK – DAY.

MARCELA sits on the grass playing with RUBEN.

In the distance is a MAN selling brightly colored balloons.

CHRISTE walks over and sits down next to her son.

                    CHRISTE
Hi, honey.

                    RUBEN
            (*delighted to see his mother*)
Mommy!

                    CHRISTE
Are you having fun with grandma?

                    RUBEN
Yes.
            (*pointing at the balloon man*)
Balloons!

                    CHRISTE
Would you like Mommy to get you a
balloon?

                    RUBEN
            (*big smile*)
Yes.

                    MARCELA
Did you talk to your boss?

CHRISTE
Yes.

MARCELA
What did he say?

CHRISTE
He's going to think about it.

MARCELA
That's great.

CHRISTE
That doesn't mean he's going to do anything.

MARCELA
Christe, don't be so negative. You have done so well in the last three years. And it hasn't been easy, raising a child by yourself.

CHRISTE
Hardly by myself, Mom.

MARCELA
Well that ex-husband of yours doesn't do anything.

CHRISTE
I wasn't talking about Manuel.

MARCELA
Me? I do nothing.

CHRISTE
You do everything.

MARCELA
(*pulling Ruben into her arms*)
Well, I can't help loving him.

RUBEN
Balloon, Grandma?

MARCELA
In a second, honey. Your mommy's going
to get you a balloon.
(*continuing her conversation
with Christe*)
I'm just so sorry you're tired all the time.
What kind of life can a young woman
have when she has to go to bed at eight
o'clock every night?

RUBEN pulls himself out his grandmother's embrace and wanders off toward BALLOON MAN.

CHRISTE
It's going to be all right. I just have to play
the game a little better.

MARCELA
What do you mean?

CHRISTE
You watch me. Tomorrow morning at six.
Bright red eye shadow.

MARCELA
(*laughing*)
What?

RUBEN starts running toward BALLOON MAN.

BALLOON MAN is about thirty yards away, his back turned toward the scampering child.

CHRISTE sees RUBEN, jumps up, and starts running after him.

She catches up with him about twenty feet away from BALLOON MAN. She grabs her son by the hands and swings him around in the air.

RUBEN squeals with delight. CHRISTE looks at BALLOON MAN.

They lock eyes for a brief second.

CHRISTE freezes in shock.

BALLOON MAN turns away.

The balloons fly into the air.

BALLOON MAN races off.

RUBEN points up into the sky as the balloons fly away.

> RUBEN
> Mommy! Mommy! Look at the balloons!

But CHRISTE is speechless.

She's seen a ghost.

INT. CHRISTE'S BEDROOM – NIGHT.

CHRISTE is asleep.

Her head rolls back and forth and her face grimaces with anxiety.

She's in the midst of a terrible nightmare.

                                                        CUT TO

CHRISTE'S DREAM.

She stands in the center aisle of a large English concert hall.

CHRISTE looks up to her left. A FOREIGN AMBASSADOR sits in a box watching the concert.

She looks to the right.

An ARAB ASSASSIN enters another box and sits down. The ASSASSIN takes a casual peek at the AMBASSADOR. He smiles.

                                                        CUT TO

CHRISTE's face.

She hears a voice say in a southern accent: *"IF YOU SAY ANYTHING TO ANYBODY, YOUR CHILD WILL DIE!"*

                                                        CUT TO

CHRISTE's POV of the orchestra.

In the last row is a TALL DISTINGUISHED MAN in a tuxedo. He is the cymbal player, and looks down at the musical score in front of him.

                                                        CUT TO

The TALL DISTINGUISHED MAN's POV:

It pans across the staff ending on a single whole note.

The TALL DISTINGUISHED MAN turns and picks up a large pair of cymbals.

He holds them up and looks up toward the CONDUCTOR.

Shooting through the cymbals, the view zooms into CHRISTE's face.

She looks back and forth from the AMBASSADOR to the ASSASSIN. Her face becoming more anguished.

CUT TO

ASSASSIN'S BOX.

The ASSASSIN places his hand inside his coat, reaching towards a hidden weapon.

CHRISTE is desperate. She looks up.

The ASSASSIN is moving forward, exposing the tip of his gun.

The CONDUCTOR looks up toward the TALL DISTINGUISHED MAN.

He raises the cymbals.

A close view of the gun now in the ASSASSIN's hand.

CHRISTE looks at the AMBASSADOR. He is thoroughly enjoying the concert, a pleased smile on his face.

The ASSASSIN's gun is poised.

His finger slowly grips the trigger.

CHRISTE clamps her hand over her mouth to keep herself from screaming.

The cymbals are held in the foreground and through them we can see the orchestra and the CONDUCTOR beyond.

The CONDUCTOR looks up from his score and points deliberately to the TALL DISTINGUISHED MAN.

The cymbals clash together as CHRISTE thrusts her hand away from her mouth, unable to stop the rising scream.

> CUT TO

INT. CHRISTE'S BEDROOM – NIGHT.

She's jolted awake by the sound of her own scream.

She stares wide-eyed around the dark room. Frightened and breathless.

> DISSOLVE TO

INT. CHRISTE'S OFFICE-MORNING

A haggard CHRISTE sits behind her desk leafing through the phone book. LUCIA VILLA walks in.

> VILLA
> So how did it go with Ramon?

> CHRISTE
> He's thinking about it.

> VILLA
> Really. Which head?

> CHRISTE
> (*smiling*)
> The little one.

> VILLA
> Very little.

VILLA turns to leave.

> CHRISTE
> Lucia, come in for a second, I want to ask you a question.

VILLA sits down in a chair across from CHRISTE'S desk.

> **VILLA**
> What's up?

> **CHRISTE**
> Did you ever go to a psychiatrist?

> **VILLA**
> Sure.

> **CHRISTE**
> What for?

> **VILLA**
> I was depressed. When I was having a lot of problems with my rock-and-roll boyfriend.

> **CHRISTE**
> Did the psychiatrist help?

> **VILLA**
> After a few sessions of bitching about my mother, I got bored. And it was getting expensive, so I got rid of the shrink, and the boyfriend, and felt a lot better. What do you need a shrink for?

> **CHRISTE**
> I've been having these terrible nightmares. Every night for the last week.

> **VILLA**
> Well, you picked a good week. They're having an international convention at the Sheraton. Every shrink in Mexico and the rest of the planet is there. I was over there yesterday and booked the world expert on eating disorders for my morning show.

CHRISTE
Do you ever have the feeling you're being followed?

VILLA
All the time.

CHRISTE
Really?

VILLA
Yeah. And I am. Look Christe, if you're on television every day, every man out there thinks you're sleeping with your boss. So when he sees you on the street he figures, "Why not me too?" So they follow you and try and pick you up. They would die to spend five minutes in you.

CHRISTE
It's not that.

VILLA
Maybe you just need some sleep.

CHRISTE
I'm afraid to go to sleep.

VILLA
Then you better see someone because you're not looking too good. And when that happens, you're history in this business.

EXT. MARIA ISABEL SHERATON – DAY.

A SLOW PAN UP THE BUILDING.

DISSOLVE TO

INT. LARGE HOTEL MEETING ROOM – DAY.

DR. NICK WOLFE, an attractive man in his early forties, stands before a lectern giving a medical paper to a group of about sixty psychiatrists.

> WOLFE
> Mysteries intrigue us all. Attempting to solve them promises an encounter with the unknown and the unexpected. A crime of passion – executed with imagination and violence – is emotionally compelling. Sometimes it gets our heart pumping faster.

Three rows back, and staring at him with utter fascination, is CHRISTE.

There's more than just intellectual interest in her large, electric-blue eyes, now made more dramatic by the liberal use of bright red eye shadow.

In fact, WOLFE finds it hard to refrain from staring back at her.

> WOLFE
> Other times it can chill us to the bone. The unexpected death, however grotesque, is spellbinding. So, too, are the tantalizing clues left for the reader to unravel, the false leads, the sudden moment of revelation and, finally, the unsuspected culprit is exposed and brought to justice.

CHRISTE gives WOLFE such a sexy, sly smile that he has to look away from her.

                    WOLFE
          Perhaps it will surprise you to learn that
          each of us is a great mystery writer. Every
          night we create our stories, filling them
          with passion and adventure and colorful
          characters – some villains, some victims,
          some witnesses. We leave ourselves
          puzzling, often disturbing clues that
          summon us to the role of detective.

He looks up from his notes.

CHRISTE is still staring at him.

                    WOLFE
          These mystery stories are, of course, our
          dreams. And it is through our dreams that
          we work over the emotional "crimes"
          perpetrated each and every day, past and
          present. The dream is a mystery that
          only the dreamer can solve. And yet, in
          the solution lies the knowledge that the
          dreamer may not wish to have.

Something dark clouds CHRISTE'S EYES. She abruptly looks away from WOLFE.
He turns back to his notes.

                    WOLFE
          Why analyze a dream in the first place?
          Does the effort give you enough reward
          to justify the time, work, and anxiety
          involved?

He looks back up.

CHRISTE is gone.

DISSOLVE TO

INT. HOTEL HOSPITALITY SUITE – DAY.

A large group of PSYCHIATRISTS sip cocktails and talk shop. DR. MARIA MATEOS, WOLFE and an old colleague of his, DR. ROSS MONTANA, are in a heated discussion.

> MONTANA
> From my experiences it refutes all conventional dream analysis theory.

> MARIA MATEOS
> C'mon, Ross. That's ridiculous.

> MONTANA
> I'm telling you Maria, you have to come to my clinic in Atlanta and see for yourself. We're working up cases where the subconscious has been erased and reprogrammed.

> MARIA MATEOS
> Do you buy this, Nick?

> WOLFE
> (*shaking his head*)
> You can't wipe clean a lifetime of experience, Ross. No matter what kind of mind-altering experiments you run. It's all there in the subconscious, whether you can find it or not. And it will ultimately emerge in the patient's dreams.

> MONTANA
> Sure it can emerge. But your so-called "lifetime experiences" can be altered and disguised.

Over MONTANA'S shoulder, WOLFE sees CHRISTE. She's again staring at him from the entrance to the suite.

> WOLFE
> (*looking past Ross*)
> I'm sure it can. Would you excuse me for a minute?

WOLFE starts walking toward CHRISTE.

She turns around in the open doorway and vanishes down the hallway.

WOLFE pushes through groups in conversation, finally reaching the doorway.

INT. HOTEL HALLWAY – DAY.

WOLFE enters the hallway. He sees CHRISTE standing in front of an elevator at the far end of the corridor.

She stares at the CLOSED ELEVATOR DOORS.

WOLFE walks down the corridor. He comes to a stop next to her, pushes the elevator button she hasn't actually pushed, and waits.

Feeling a little awkward about exactly what to say, WOLFE finally turns to CHRISTE, only to hear MARIA calling his name.

> MARIA MATEOS
> (*standing in the doorway to the suite*)
> Nick, where are you going?

> WOLFE
> (*thinking fast*)
> I was going down to the lobby to make a call.

The elevator doors open.

CHRISTE steps in, turns around and stares back, her eyes meeting WOLFE's.

>### MARIA MATEOS
>Why don't you use the phone here?

>### WOLFE
>Where?

CHRISTE opens her handbag and reaches into it.

WOLFE sees the glint of a WHITE PAPER ENVELOPE before the elevator doors start to close.

He looks up at CHRISTE's face.
Her lips slowly part as though she's about to say something.

>### WOLFE
>*(eyes on Christe but still*
>*talking to Maria)*
>There's a phone there?

The elevator doors shut. CHRISTE is gone again.

>### MARIA MATEOS
>Yes. It's in the other room. I'll show you.

Covering his disappointment with a smile, WOLFE turns toward MARIA and walks back up the hallway.

EXT. MARIA ISABEL SHERATON – DAY.

WOLFE, carrying a Mexico City guidebook, exits the hotel and walks down the boulevard.

Across the street is CHRISTE. She follows him.

EXT. MUSEUM OF ANTHROPOLOGY – DAY.

WOLFE walks up the steps and goes inside. CHRISTE follows.

INT. MUSEUM – DAY.

WOLFE stands before a huge circular Aztec calendar, reading from his guidebook. The calendar reminds him of something and he takes out his appointment book. He crosses out a two o'clock appointment.

He slips the book back into his jacket and suddenly realizes that CHRISTE is standing right next to him.

> WOLFE
> (*turns to her*)
> Haven't I seen you before?

> CHRISTE
> (*seductive smile*)
> That's not very original.

> WOLFE
> (*smiling back*)
> I'm not trying to be original. I'm trying to be accurate.

> CHRISTE
> Possibly.

> WOLFE
> The lecture yesterday. You were there.

> CHRISTE
> Yes.

> WOLFE
> Are you interested in dream analysis?

She looks over her shoulder.

A short, DARK MAN has entered the deserted gallery.

She studies the man carefully then turns back to WOLFE.

> CHRISTE
> I'm interested in you.

> WOLFE
> Why?

> CHRISTE
> (*shoving an envelope in his hand*)
> We can't talk here. I have a very jealous husband.

She quickly walks away. WOLFE watches her leave the gallery.

He looks over to the DARK MAN, who seems to have frightened CHRISTE away.

He's intensely studying a mural.

WOLFE looks down at the ENVELOPE in his hand. It's the same one that was in CHRISTE's handbag at the elevator.

He rips it open. In it is a Sheraton room key.

There is also a slip of paper. On it is written:

> MEET ME IN ROOM 113 AT NOON
> TOMORROW. YOU WON'T BE
> DISAPPOINTED.

INT. WOLFE'S HOTEL ROOM – EARLY THE NEXT MORNING.

WOLFE lies in bed reading. He has had a restless night. He looks over at the room key resting on the bedside table.

He picks it up, studies it for a second, then flips it into a waste basket.

He looks at his watch. It's six in the morning.

He picks up his remote control and presses it. The television set across the room clicks on.

He looks at the screen and his mouth drops.

It's CHRISTE reading the morning news.

CUT TO

INT. HOTEL ROOM – NOON.

WOLFE sits in a chair. Waiting. He looks at his watch. It's a little past noon.

The door opens and CHRISTE walks in.

She closes the door, locks it, and hooks the chain. She turns around to face WOLFE.

> WOLFE
> Hello, Mrs. Rivera.

> CHRISTE
> (*panicky*)
> How did you know my name?

> WOLFE
> I saw you on the news this morning.

CHRISTE
(*relieved*)
Oh, that.
(*suspicious*)
Nobody has talked to you about me, have they?

WOLFE
No.

CHRISTE
Good. Would you like something to drink?

WOLFE
No, thank you. So what are we doing here?

CHRISTE
There's going to be an assassination.

WOLFE
Why don't you call the police?

CHRISTE
Because it hasn't happened yet.

WOLFE
How do you know it's going to happen?

CHRISTE
Because I keep dreaming about it.

WOLFE
Now all of this is making a little sense. You got me here because my specialty is dream analysis. But why the seduction routine? You just had to make appointment and come to…

CHRISTE
I couldn't do that. I think I'm being followed. If I was seen with you, they'd find out who you are. And your life would be in danger.

WOLFE
Why don't you let me worry about that.

CHRISTE
You don't believe me?

WOLFE
Of course I believe you. I would just like to know more. Who's going to put my life in danger?

CHRISTE
The Arabs.

WOLFE
I see. Let's go back a little bit. Tell me about your dream.

CHRISTE
I'm in a concert hall. The orchestra is playing. There's an important ambassador there. Somehow I know there's a plot to assassinate him but I can't tell anybody because they've kidnapped my little boy. I see an assassin sitting in a box. He's about to shoot when…

WOLFE
The cymbals clash.

CHRISTE
Yes. That's right. How did you know that?

                    WOLFE
            (*searching his memory*)
I don't know. I just remembered it from
somewhere.

                    CHRISTE
Looks like I found the perfect doctor. He
has the same nightmares I do.

                    WOLFE
Let's hope not. Go on.

                    CHRISTE
So the assassin aims the gun at the
ambassador. He's about to pull the trigger.
When the cymbal clashes, I scream and
wake up.
            (*shaking her head*)
It doesn't make much sense, does it?

                    WOLFE
On the surface, dreams are created to
make no sense. If they did, you wouldn't
have them. I need more information. Tell
me about your jealous husband.

                    CHRISTE
Ex-husband. And he isn't jealous. I made
that part up.

                    WOLFE
Where do you live?

                    CHRISTE
In an apartment with my mother and my
son, Ruben. He's three.

                    WOLFE
Were you born here?

CHRISTE
Yes.

WOLFE
What did your father do?

CHRISTE
He was an American. Working here for the State Department. He met my mother, they got married and, after I was born, moved to Virginia. That's where my father comes from originally. It was great there, I had a lot of American friends at school, and then, when I was about fifteen, my mother left him and we returned to Mexico City.

WOLFE
What happened to him?

CHRISTE
He left the government and went to work for Bacon Telecommunications in the Mid-East.

WOLFE
Bacon? The crazy Georgia billionaire that lost the election?

CHRISTE
Yes, and it looks like he's going to run again.

WOLFE
You never saw your father again?

CHRISTE
No. He died in a terrorist explosion.

WOLFE
Why did you break up with your husband?

CHRISTE
Because Manuel said Ruben wasn't his son.

WOLFE
Wasn't he?

CHRISTE
No.

WOLFE
Who was the father?

CHRISTE
I don't know.
(she stops, not wanting to go on, then, emphatically)
I never should have had a child!

WOLFE
Why?

CHRISTE
Because. He. Is. Going. To. Be. Kidnapped.

WOLFE
But that's in your dream.

CHRISTE
It doesn't make any difference. It's going to happen anyway.

WOLFE
You think your dream… is some kind of premonition?

CHRISTE
I guess so.

WOLFE
Who's going to kidnap your child?

CHRISTE
An English couple. I meet them in Marrakesh. But there is an Arab too. He's going to shoot the ambassador.

WOLFE
An Arab?

CHRISTE
Yes.

WOLFE
Do you know any Arabs?

CHRISTE
Do I know any Arabs?
(bitterly)
Intimately. They abducted me in Beirut four years ago. I was rescued. By a U.S. commando team.

WOLFE
(thinking back)
Oh. Yes. I remember. Around '91, '92? How long were you a hostage?

CHRISTE
Six months. I don't remember any of it.

WOLFE
Why not?

CHRISTE
I was drugged. Hypnotized. Brainwashed. That's what they told me.

WOLFE
Who told you?

CHRISTE
Some Intelligence guys. They put me under observation for six weeks after I was rescued, and found nothing. It's like one big blank to me.

WOLFE
But now you're dreaming about it?

CHRISTE
No. Nothing about being a hostage. Just the assassination.

WOLFE
(trying to make some sense out of Christe's confused story)
So the English couple takes your child to keep you from telling the police?

CHRISTE
I would tell the police in a minute. What the hell do I care about some diplomat? But my husband won't let me.

WOLFE
Your husband?

CHRISTE
In the dream I have a husband.

WOLFE
When did you get married?

CHRISTE
I don't know.

WOLFE
I don't mean your dream husband.

CHRISTE
Oh. About five years ago.

WOLFE
Before Beirut.

CHRISTE
Yes.

WOLFE
Did you and Manuel ever want children?

CHRISTE
Oh sure.

WOLFE
What changed your mind?

CHRISTE
I don't know. I just felt if I had a child… it would be kidnapped.

WOLFE
When did you feel this?

CHRISTE
(*thinking*)
When I got back from Beirut.

WOLFE
So something changed.

CHRISTE

Yes.

WOLFE

After you were a hostage?

CHRISTE

Yes.

WOLFE

They did something to you?

CHRISTE
(*bitterly*)
They certainly did. And I have Ruben to prove it. It was hard on my macho husband. He tried to forget what happened to me but the older Ruben got the more Arabic he looked. After a few years I got tired of feeling guilty for something I couldn't even remember, so we broke up.
(*shaking her head*)
Does this make any sense at all?

WOLFE

Sure. But I need more information. Especially about your dream. I want you to keep a tape recorder by your bedside so that the next time you have the dream you can record your memories of it immediately after you wake up. The longer you wait? The most important information will be forgotten.

CHRISTE

Then you're going to help me?

WOLFE
Yes. But let's stop for now. Next time I want you to come to an office. I have a friend here who…

CHRISTE
I can't do that. I won't put you in danger.

WOLFE
Okay, we'll meet here for now.
   (he takes out his appointment book)
How about Friday, same time?

CHRISTE
That will be fine. Thank you.

WOLFE
By the way, when did you start having the dream?

CHRISTE
Last month.

WOLFE
Anything happen that was unusual?

CHRISTE
Yes. I thought I saw my father in the park. He was selling balloons.

DISSOLVE TO

INT. CHRISTE'S BEDROOM – THAT NIGHT.

CHRISTE lies on her back in bed, asleep. On the bedside table is a small cassette recorder.

CHRISTE is dreaming.

CUT TO

CHRISTE'S DREAM.

CHRISTE is standing on a treadmill.

On her head, covering her eyes and ears, is a headset. A thick cord of wires is plugged into the back. They snake down CHRISTE'S shoulder and are plugged into a computer resting on the floor to the right of the treadmill.

On the screen of the computer is what CHRISTE sees in the headset.

It's a virtual reality projection of an opera hall. If she looks straight ahead, she sees a computer-generated picture of the audience in the orchestra seats and the opera boxes directly above them.

In the center box is a computer-animated figure of the PRESIDENT.

She hears PRINCE CHARMING's voice in her head, the distinctive southern accent.

> PRINCE CHARMING
> AMBROSE CHAPEL.

Her head jerks.

The voice again.

> PRINCE CHARMING
> AIM THE GUN AT THE PRESIDENT!

CHRISTE obeys like a programmed robot.

She raises her hand.

In it is an electronic gun.

She points the gun at the computer-generated figure of the PRESIDENT sitting in the opera box.

The voice again.

> PRINCE CHARMING
> SHOOT THE PRESIDENT!

She presses the trigger.

There's a sound of a shot as part of the opera box explodes in an electronic puff of smoke to the PRESIDENT's left.

CHRISTE has missed her target.

The voice again.

> PRINCE CHARMING
> AIM THE GUN AT THE PRESIDENT.

CHRISTE aims again, moving a few degrees to the right.

The voice again.

> PRINCE CHARMING
> SHOOT THE PRESIDENT!

She presses the trigger again.

There's a second electronic gunshot sound.

This time CHRISTE is on the mark and the computer-generated image of the PRESIDENT falls back dead.

The voice again.

> PRINCE CHARMING
> YOU WILL REMEMBER NOTHING.

CHRISTE nods her head.

Next on the screen is a concert hall

It cuts to a computer image of a BLONDE WOMAN standing in the aisle.

Her face is filled with anxiety.

The image freezes.

The voice again.

> PRINCE CHARMING
> YOU ARE THIS WOMAN. THEY
> HAVE KIDNAPPED YOUR CHILD.
> IF YOU SAY ANYTHING ABOUT
> WHAT YOU'RE PLANNING TO
> DO... YOU WILL NEVER SEE
> YOUR CHILD AGAIN! DO YOU
> UNDERSTAND ME!

CHRISTE nods.

The voice again.

> PRINCE CHARMING
> NOW WATCH THIS AND
> REMEMBER IT!

The image unfreezes.

The BLONDE WOMAN has morphed into CHRISTE.

CHRISTE looks to the left, and there's the AMBASSADOR sitting in his box.

She looks to the right and again the ASSASSIN enters his box, sits down, and looks over at the AMBASSADOR.

CUT TO

CHRISTE's face.

It fills with anxiety.

She looks at the orchestra onstage.

The CYMBAL PLAYER raises the cymbals.

The ASSASSIN's gun is poised to fire.

CHRISTE covers her mouth with her hand.

The cymbals clash together and CHRISTE screams.

CUT TO

INT. CHRISTE'S BEDROOM - NIGHT.

Again CHRISTE awakens to the sound of her own scream.

She takes a second to get her bearings.

Then she picks up the cassette recorder from the bedside table and starts talking into it.

CUT TO

INT. LOBBY MEXICO CITY SHERATON – DAY.

CHRISTE waits at a busy bank of elevators. The doors before her open and a large group of noisy tourists piles out into the lobby.

CHRISTE gets into the vacant car and is quickly surrounded.

The elevator fills and the doors are just about to close when a tall, swarthy man with MIRRORED SUNGLASSES steps inside.

INT. ELEVATOR – DAY.

The car heads upward. At each stop, people get off until the elevator is empty except for CHRISTE and MIRRORED SUNGLASSES.

CHRISTE looks over at him. He looks back at her.

The eleventh floor.

The elevator doors slide open and CHRISTE gets out.

MIRRORED SUNGLASSES follows.

INT. HOTEL CORRIDOR – DAY.

CHRISTE walks down the hall.

MIRRORED SUNGLASSES walks behind her. He's about thirty feet away when CHRISTE stops.

MIRRORED SUNGLASSES also stops.

CHRISTE adjusts her skirt, taking a peek over her shoulder.

MIRRORED SUNGLASSES pretends he's looking for a room number.

At the far end of the hallway a door opens, and a YOUNG MEXICAN COUPLE emerges. They walk down the hall, stop before the elevator and push the down button.

CHRISTE, now suspicious, proceeds down the hall a little further, stopping one door before ROOM 113.

She pretends to search in her purse for her room key. She sneaks another peak at MIRRORED SUNGLASSES.

He is watching her.

The elevator doors open. The YOUNG COUPLE walks inside.

CHRISTE abruptly turns around, racing past MIRRORED SUNGLASSES, and jumps inside the elevator.

MIRRORED SUNGLASSES moves after her, but the elevator doors close just before he reaches them.

He turns away, smiling to himself.

INT. HOTEL ROOM – DAY.

WOLFE stands by a window, waiting for CHRISTE. The phone rings. He picks it up.

                    WOLFE
Hello.

                    CHRISTE
                  (*on the phone*)
Dr. Wolfe, it's me. A man followed me up to your floor. I lost him but we can't meet there. Meet me in the subway at Residencia Polanco. Get on the west bound platform. You'll see me get on the train.

                    WOLFE
Are you sure you were followed?

                    CHRISTE
                  (*on the phone*)
Yes. Hurry!

The line goes dead. WOLFE takes a deep breath and slowly hangs up the phone. What has he gotten himself into? A crazy paranoid who insists on having therapy sessions on the subway?

He shakes his head but walks toward the door.

INT. SUBWAY CAR - DAY.

Close shot. A headset. We pull back to see WOLFE listening to CHRISTE's cassette recorder.

They sit next to each other on a moving subway train. The car is packed with midday commuters.

Through his earphones, WOLFE hears:

>   CHRISTE
>   (*her breathless voice coming
>   from the recorder*)
>   I couldn't let him be shot so I screamed
>   out... and then I woke up.

WOLFE switches off the recorder and slips off the earphones.

>   WOLFE
>   Is that everything you remember?

>   CHRISTE
>   No, there was another part, when I shoot.
>   Oh... I can't remember...

>   WOLFE
>   You think you remember shooting
>   someone, but then you forget it?

>   CHRISTE
>   Yes. It's like when I try to remember the
>   shooting part I suddenly turn into that
>   blonde woman watching the assassin.

WOLFE
(*cutting her off*)
But what about the part before you become the blonde woman?

CHRISTE

Yes.
   (*then when she tries to remember*)
No. No. No. The more I try to remember, the more I think *I'm* the blonde woman. And then I hear this man's voice in my head.
   (*imitating Prince Charming's voice*)
"If you say anything to anybody, your child will die!"

WOLFE

Who's that?

CHRISTE

Who's what?

WOLFE

You just said something in a southern accent.

CHRISTE

What did I say?

WOLFE

(*imitating Christe's southern accent*)
"If you say anything to anybody, your child will die!"

CHRISTE
   (*suddenly fearful*)
You sound like my father!

WOLFE

You heard your father in your dream?

CHRISTE
(*trying to remember*)
Yes, saying just what you said.

WOLFE
(*repeating*)
"If you say anything to anybody, your child will die!"

CHRISTE
(*more fearful*)
STOP SAYING THAT!

A couple of MEXICAN WORKERS look at them.

WOLFE
What's the matter?

CHRISTE
MY CHILD WILL DIE!
(*starting to get up*)
I can't talk about this anymore.

WOLFE
Why?

CHRISTE
(*very upset*)
Because Ruben will die!

More looks from the passengers. CHRISTE stands up to leave.

WOLFE
Okay Christe. I understand. We're not going to talk about it anymore. I promise. Now will you please sit down.

CHRISTE
I have to go.

WOLFE
Just give me a few more minutes.
(*looking around*)
And couldn't we go to a little less public place?

CHRISTE
(*realizing they're in a group of staring passengers*)
Okay. And you won't ask me any more questions?

WOLFE
No. Christe, you've got to trust me.

CHRISTE sits back down next to the doctor.

CHRISTE
(*still not convinced*)
What are we going to talk about?

WOLFE
Anything you want.

CHRISTE
(*the panic subsides*)
Okay. Let's talk about you.

EXT. COFFEE SHOP OVERLOOKING THE CITY – DAY.

WOLFE and CHRISTE sit at a table, drinking coffee.

WOLFE
Now, let's see you do your Barbara Walters.

CHRISTE
Okay.
(*warming to the challenge*)
Where do you live?

WOLFE
Chicago.

CHRISTE
Are you married?

WOLFE
Divorced.

CHRISTE
What happened?

WOLFE
My wife thought I got too involved with my patients and didn't have enough time for her.

CHRISTE
Did you?

WOLFE
Not really, but it's hard to leave your work in the office.

CHRISTE
What made you become a psychiatrist?

WOLFE
I like to help people.

CHRISTE
(*imitating Barbara Walters*)
Oh doctor, you can do better than that.

WOLFE
It makes me feel good? Worthwhile?

CHRISTE
Ah. A Mother Teresa complex!

WOLFE
The pay's a little better.

CHRISTE
Do you have a girlfriend?

WOLFE
I have "old girlfriends."

CHRISTE
What's that mean?

WOLFE
Women I used to go out with, who know me very well and don't expect too much.

CHRISTE
Do you sleep with them?

WOLFE
Sometimes.

CHRISTE
But nothing more than that?

WOLFE
It's enough for me.

CHRISTE
Is it enough for them?

WOLFE
Probably not, but that's the best I can do for now.

CHRISTE
Haven't you ever been in love?

WOLFE
Oh yes.

CHRISTE
And wasn't it great?

WOLFE
Yes and no.

CHRISTE
We only have time for the "yes" part.

WOLFE
(*smiling*)
Okay. First it's that look in her eyes. It burns right through you. The fevered anticipation. The first time your fingers touch. The smell of her hair. The feel of her body pressing against yours. And then the first kiss. Oh God. If there could only just be one. But, of course, there can't. And then you drown in those kisses.

CHRISTE
You'd drown if you kissed me?

WOLFE
Just a figure of speech.

CHRISTE
Why don't we just try it? I forget the last time I was kissed.

WOLFE
It's unethical.

                    CHRISTE
I don't mind.

                    WOLFE
You don't have to mind. But I do.

                    CHRISTE
Because you're the doctor.

                    WOLFE
That's right. And you're the patient.

                    CHRISTE
Too bad. You're the first man I've even thought about kissing. Ever since Beirut, I haven't felt very sexy.

                    WOLFE
I don't think being sexy is the problem.

                    CHRISTE
No?

                    WOLFE
You're very sexy Christe. There's just nothing intimate about it.

                    CHRISTE
You mean like a Barbie doll?

                    WOLFE
Not exactly. You want to be touched. You just can't be now.

                    CHRISTE
How do you know that?

WOLFE
Remember your seduction routine? You went through the motions. Like a pro. But there was no surrender in it.

CHRISTE
What am I supposed to do? Lie down and spread my legs?

WOLFE
Making love is opening up for both a man and a woman. What's better than to surrender in your lover's arms?

CHRISTE
I don't even know what you're talking about.
(*sighing*)
I'm just a tight-assed neurotic with a recurring nightmare.

WOLFE
Don't lose heart. We'll figure it out. We made a lot of progress today. But I need more background, so what I would like you to do is talk to your mother.

CHRISTE
About what?

WOLFE
About why you father left.

CHRISTE
I told you.

WOLFE
I know. But that was years ago. Maybe now that you're older, she'll tell you more.

INT. LARRY KING SHOW – NIGHT.

JAY JEFFERSON KEEN stands beside a live TV camera. He's six-six, bald, and built like a cobra ready to strike. His eyes are hooded and he has a disarming alligator grin.

His spin doctor, HARLEN SPECTOR, walks over and whispers something in his ear. SPECTOR is a bright young ferret of a man. KEEN smiles at SPECTOR and turns back to the stage.

There, LARRY KING is questioning MAJOR JOHN BACON. Everyone calls him MAJOR and it's not because it's his rank. He's a small man with an ego ten feet tall. A self-made billionaire, he is used to getting what he wants. Even the presidency of the United States.

> KING
> So, do you think, then, the pollsters are reading it wrong, not getting it right? I mean, you're a sharp businessman.

> MAJOR
> Just wait 'til next week.

> KING
> Why wait? You can announce your candidacy, right now, live on my show.

> MAJOR
> Just hold on there, Larry. I am not getting into this race until I'm absolutely sure the people really need me.

> KING
> But according to the polls, if the election were held today, you get beaten worse than you did in '92.

MAJOR
(*smiling*)
You know Larry, I just love everyday people. A guy in a little country town the other day came up to me and asked me a question. He says, "Major, have you ever had a pollster call you at home?" I said, "No." He said, "I've called all over town. I can't find anybody that's ever talked to a pollster, I guess they miss a lot." And he's the kind of American that's going to be voting for me if I do get into this race.

KING
And I bet you think there's a whole lot of them too?

MAJOR
You bet.

KING
(*turning to the camera*)
We'll be back with Major Bacon. Is he in the race, or not? We'll try to get him to tell us in the next half hour. And we'll include your phone calls. Don't go away.

The show goes off the air. KEEN walks onto the set.

KEEN
Great show, Larry.

KING
Major is always a great show.

King stands up and stretches.

KING
(*calling to the sound man*)
Unhook me a second. I got to walk this off.
(*to Major*)
My foot fell asleep.

MAJOR
(*laughing*)
I told you I was boring. Maybe you didn't know it, but you can't fool a fool.

Smiling, KING walks away from the desk. MAJOR motions to KEEN and SPECTOR. They walk over. MAJOR whispers in KEEN's EAR.

MAJOR
So when am I getting into this election?

KEEN
When you made me campaign manager, you said one thing, remember? "Just made sure I win and I don't care how."

MAJOR
That's right.

KEEN
And I said, "The cat's in the bag and the bag's in the river," but don't ask me who put her there.

MAJOR
Okay. I made you a promise. But I don't like flying blind, son. It's not my style.

SPECTOR
It takes more than style to get into the White House.

MAJOR
But, boys, we've got to get this show on the road.

SPECTOR
You have to enter the election at the right dramatic moment. Timing is everything. And I just got some good news from inside the president's campaign.

MAJOR
What?

SPECTOR
It's definite. He's going to the Opera. In Mexico City.

MAJOR
So?

KEEN
This could be the place.

SPECTOR
And the time.

INT. CHRISTE'S OFFICE.

She sits behind her desk talking on the phone.

CHRISTE
Mom, I'm going to try and get home early tonight. No. No. Don't cook anything special. Just put Ruben to bed, and I'll see you later.

She hangs up the phone. Her boss, LUIS RAMON, walks in the office.

RAMON
What have you done about Bassene?

CHRISTE
We've been missing each other.

RAMON
I just got off the phone with him. He still wants you.

CHRISTE
You mean he wants to go after my bones.

RAMON
C'mon. You're a big girl, you can handle him.

CHRISTE
I don't want to handle him. I don't want to be within ten miles of him.

RAMON
Hey, don't give me a hard time, just do it!

CHRISTE
Just answer one question for me. You've already delivered my ass on this one, haven't you, Luis?

RAMON
What are you talking about?

CHRISTE
You've already set up the interview?

RAMON
Yeah, so what? I'm a producer. That's what I'm supposed to do.

CHRISTE
You mean you're a pimp. *Where* am I
supposed to do it?

RAMON
At his apartment.

CHRISTE
Day or night?

RAMON
Friday. Night.

CHRISTE
What time?

RAMON
Nine o'clock.

CHRISTE
Sounds like a good job of pimping to me.

RAMON
What's he going to do? Fuck you in front
of the cameraman?

RAMON slams out of CHRISTE's office.

INT. KITCHEN – NIGHT.

CHRISTE sits across a breakfast table from her MOTHER.

CHRISTE
I wanted to talk to you because I've been
having some problems.

MARCELA
What kind of problems?

CHRISTE
Bad dreams. Very upsetting. I think I'm being followed. I worry about Ruben all the time.

MARCELA
What about Ruben?

CHRISTE
I just have this feeling he's in danger. I want you to take him to Uncle Miguel's. He'll be safe there.

MARCELA
But I can't stand that wife of his. She keeps a house like a museum. I'm afraid to sit in her precious living room. I might disturb something.

CHRISTE
I know, Mom. She's impossible. But you're going to have to put up with her for a few days. I'm sorry. I know I'm acting crazy. I went to see a doctor.

MARCELA
What did he say?

CHRISTE
We're kind of stuck. He says he needs more information. About my childhood.

MARCELA
Like what?

CHRISTE
Like why you and dad broke up.

MARCELA
What does that have to do with anything?

CHRISTE
In my dream I keep hearing Daddy telling
me things.

MARCELA
(*suddenly very suspicious*)
What kind of things?

CHRISTE
Daddy says, "If I say anything, to... "

She stops, grimacing with pain.

MARCELA
(*concerned*)
What's the matter?

CHRISTE
I just said something to somebody.

MARCELA
So?

CHRISTE
I suddenly got this pounding headache.
I can't talk about this anymore.

MARCELA
I'll get you some aspirin.

INT. HOTEL RESTAURANT - NIGHT.

WOLFE is discussing CHRISTE's case over dinner with
DR. ROSS MONTANA.

MONTANA
Given the fact that she was a hostage
for six months, and the Intelligence
guys found nothing but a blanked-out
memory, it seems like a good possibility

that she was a guinea pig for some kind of mind control experiment. Especially since when she tries to remember the first part of her dream she experiences a tremendous amount of anxiety and remembers something else. Sounds like mis-addressing to me.

WOLFE
Mis-addressing?

MONTANA
It's a mind control technique to cover up programmed instructions. You give the conscious mind the address of a false memory.

WOLFE
So all this stuff about the ambassador being shot could be a cover for something else?

MONTANA
That's right. The problem with hypnotic programming is that it always leaks out into the subconscious. There's no way to absolutely contain it. That's why she's having all these mixed-up nightmares. You may have a Sleeping Beauty on your hands.

WOLFE
A Sleeping Beauty?

MONTANA
A programed assassin. One of the well-kept secrets of the CIA. I heard they ran some experiments in the early Eighties parceled out to private venders, real hush-

hush stuff. The only reason I know about it is that they had a couple of burnouts that they dumped in my clinic. I thought it was strange we were getting all these similar cases, and when I checked their records, I found they all came from the same hospital in Virginia.

WOLFE
What could Christe be programmed to do?

MONTANA
Blow up a building. A plane. Assassinate somebody. Maybe she's being run by that Shiite terrorist group? Wasn't she on television saying that the president has to pay for all those Arabs he killed?

WOLFE
Yes. But she was doped up. She didn't know what she was saying.

MONTANA
And she's not going to know what she's doing when she shoots someone either.

WOLFE
But what can I do?

MONTANA
Nothing. This isn't your normal vanilla neurotic with some bad dreams, this is a time bomb just waiting to be kissed.

WOLFE
Kissed?

MONTANA
That's hypno-jargon for waking her up and putting her to work. But that's not your problem.

WOLFE
What do you mean?

MONTANA
Look doctor, you're a psychiatrist, not a member of the "American Mind Police." You should refer her to a good de-programmer and gracefully bow out.

WOLFE
I can't do that.

MONTANA
Why not?

WOLFE
I don't think, at this stage, she would trust anybody else.

MONTANA
(*studying Nick's face carefully*)
Are you getting involved with this woman?

WOLFE
I don't think so. I'm just very concerned.

MONTANA
Then get her to the right doctor! And that's not you.

WOLFE
I hear what you're saying, Ross. But I'd like one more session with her. Is there

any good test to absolutely determine that's she's been programmed?

MONTANA
Well. You can try hypnotizing her and looking for the kiss word. You know she's like a computer that needs a password. Once you hit it, she should open right up.

WOLFE
Then what?

MONTANA
Call me tomorrow. I'll do some research around here and find her the right doctor. Then, if he concurs with us, we better get the CIA in on this.

WOLFE
The CIA?

MONTANA
That's right, Nick. And we've got to move fast. Did you see the papers today? The president is coming to town.

INT. CHRISTE'S BEDROOM – NIGHT.

She lies on her back in bed. MARCELA presses a cold compress to her forehead.

MARCELA
Feel better?

CHRISTE
Thanks Mom.

MARCELA sighs deeply and then slowly starts to speak.

MARCELA
I left your father because he was sleeping around.

CHRISTE
With who?

MARCELA
Oh, I don't remember who. There were millions of young nurses at the hospital.

CHRISTE
What hospital?

MARCELA
Where your father worked.

CHRISTE
You never told me he worked at a hospital.

MARCELA
Well, he didn't always work there. It was just where he was assigned in Virginia.

CHRISTE
Assigned. By who?

MARCELA
The government.

CHRISTE
What part of the government?

MARCELA
Some secret part. He never said which.

CHRISTE
You mean he was some kind of spy?

MARCELA
He never used that word.

CHRISTE
Well, what did you think?

MARCELA
I wasn't allowed to think about that. He wouldn't have told me the truth anyway.

CHRISTE
You mean you were married to this man for over sixteen years and you didn't know what he did?

MARCELA
Oh no. He told me a million things. Just none of them were true. We were in a car accident once. While you were still a baby. I broke my arm. The pain was unbearable. He hypnotized me and told me I would feel nothing. The next thing I remembered was waking up in the hospital with a cast on. That was the only way I found out he had some kind of psychological training.

CHRISTE
(*sarcastic*)
And you left him because of "another woman?"

MARCELA
(*turning away from her daughter*)
Yes.

CHRISTE
Mom. Look at me. Are you telling me the truth?

MARCELA remains silent.

CHRISTE
Did it have something to do with me?

MARCELA
I don't want to talk about this anymore.

CHRISTE
Mom, we have to. It's screwing up my life.

MARCELA
(*extremely upset*)
I'm sorry honey. I did the best I could. I was terrified of him. When I ran away, I was sure he was going to come after us and kill me.

CHRISTE
Why?

MARCELA
(*bitterly*)
Because I took you away from him.

CHRISTE
It must have hurt him. I was hurt too. I missed him terribly.

MARCELA
(*bitterly*)
I bet you did.

CHRISTE
What do you mean by that?

MARCELA
Nothing.

CHRISTE
No, mother, it isn't "nothing."
(incredulous)
Were you jealous of me?

MARCELA
(defensive)
Why should I be?

CHRISTE
Because he spoiled me. I remember every night him coming into my room and reading to me. Sleeping Beauty was our favorite story.

MARCELA
(bursting out with long suppressed anger)
He was obsessed with you! It was sick! What was he doing in your bedroom every night? For hours and hours. Sometimes all night long!

CHRISTE
He was never in my room all night.

MARCELA
How would you know? You never remembered anything. Just like I didn't remember my broken arm. I had to find out what he was doing. So I tried to listen at your door. But he caught me. He said what you and he were doing was "top secret." I laughed in his face. "Is that what you call the things you do with your daughter at night?" He hit me. Hard. When I woke up the next morning, he was gone. I took you and left. I never want to see that man again.

CUT TO

EXT. GOLF COURSE – DAY

MAJOR stands at the edge of the green, lining up a put. Across from him, on the far side of the hole, are KEEN and SPECTOR.

>SPECTOR
>(*whispering to Keen*)
>I had an interesting chat with Prince Charming.

>KEEN
>(*whispering back*)
>Did he tell you the kiss?

>SPECTOR
>(*whispering*)
>No. I don't think he trusts us.

>KEEN
>(*whispering back*)
>He's no fool. He knows once he's completed the contract, he's nothing but a dangerous liability.

MAJOR hits his ball. It rolls past the hole stopping next to SPECTOR's ball. MAJOR strides over to KEEN.

>MAJOR
>I can't hear a goddamn word you two are saying.

>KEEN
>We're trying to keep our voices down. This conversation could be dangerous.

MAJOR
Will you stop being so melodramatic.
Nobody's going to hear what you're
saying out here.

SPECTOR reaches down and picks the golf ball up from the grass. He holds it up in front of MAJOR's face.

SPECTOR
This could be bugged.

MAJOR grabs the ball out of his hand, drops it on the green, and smashes it down the runway.

MAJOR
Feel better now?

SPECTOR
No. That was my ball.

MAJOR
*(pulling another ball
out of his pocket)*
Here's another one. Now what's going
on?

KEEN
Everything's set. We're going to announce
your candidacy.

MAJOR
When?

KEEN
Friday night. In Mexico City.

MAJOR
What?

EXT. OPERA HOUSE – NIGHT.

PRINCE CHARMING slowly walks around El Palacio de Bellas Artes, Mexico City's opera house.

He studies each entrance and exit.

Because of the late hour, the main front entrance is completely locked. There's a sign directing any late-night deliveries to the rear.

PRINCE CHARMING walks around to the back of the building.

At the rear of the opera house, PRINCE CHARMING finds a secluded area filled with trees that faces the three rear exits.

He opens a small bag he is carrying and removes a camcorder.

He lashes the camcorder to the trunk of a tree and positions it to frame the three rear exits. He adjusts the foliage around the tree so that it completely conceals the camera without obstructing its view.

He pushes the camcorder record button and walks away.

                                                DISSOLVE TO

EXT. OPERA HOUSE – DAWN.

PRINCE CHARMING returns to the rear of the opera. He unties the camcorder from the tree and slips it into his bag.

                                                DISSOLVE TO

INT. CHEAP HOTEL ROOM – DAY.

PRINCE CHARMING is viewing on a TV set the videotape recorded on the camcorder.

On the television screen is the view of the three rear exits of the opera house. He holds a remote in his hand. His finger is pressed down on the fast-forward button. At the bottom of the screen a time notation whizzes by.

A few SECURITY GUARDS enter and exit in fast motion at midnight. The next three hours there is no activity. At about 4am, a NIGHT WATCHMEN spins from door to door as he checks to see if they are locked and secure. He exits screen left and the rear of the opera is quiet once again.

At 4.10am, an OVERWEIGHT MAN in a floor-length trench coat walks up to the far right exit door, pulls a long gold keychain from his pocket, inserts a shiny brass key, opens the door and enters the building.

One hour passes and then the man emerges from the same door. He walks toward camera, stops, takes out a cigarette, and lights it.

PRINCE CHARMING freezes the videotape and zooms into the face of the man smoking the cigarette.

It is JULIO BASSENE, opera director.

DISSOLVE TO

BINOCULAR POV OF JULIO BASSENE.

Bassene racing around his magnificent high-rise apartment preparing for a seduction. His mouth moves as he sings *Tosca*.

The binocular view is from a building across the street., where PRINCE CHARMING is also singing *Tosca* into a cassette recorder sitting on the window ledge in front of him.

PRINCE CHARMING's binocular view pans back and forth as Bassene moves from the bedroom to the living room to foyer and back again.

Finally, Bassene stops abruptly, as if he's heard something and walks to the foyer. A door opens and CHRISTE and her TWO-MAN CAMERA CREW enter the apartment.

PRINCE CHARMING's rhythmic breathing suddenly halts as he watches his Sleeping Beauty being ushered into the living room and sitting on the couch.

Bassene plops down right next to her and gives CHRISTE a familiar pat on the thigh.

PRINCE CHARMING reads CHRISTE's lips as she speaks.

> PRINCE CHARMING
> "Thank you, wouldn't you feel a little more comfortable over there?"

CHRISTE points to an armchair opposite her.

> CUT TO

INT. BASSENE APARTMENT – NIGHT.

> BASSENE
> This will be just fine.

> CHRISTE
> (*laughing*)
> I'm sure, but I have to sit opposite you for the interview.

She points to the two young men holding a television camera, tripod and the lights.

> BASSENE
> We're going to do the interview now?

CHRISTE
Yes, Mr. Bassene. Didn't my office explain to you?

He gets up and starts pacing.

BASSENE
Isn't it a shame and I have so much news. Both presidents have accepted my invitation!

CHRISTE
That's wonderful. As soon as the guys get the camera up, I want you to tell me what this means to you.

BASSENE
I can't be filmed now. Not in the state I'm in. Do you know where I was last night?

CHRISTE
No?

BASSENE
The opera. I woke up in the middle of the night. My muse was speaking to me. It's four o'clock in the morning and she refuses to let me sleep. "What do you want?" I say. "Let me sleep. Let me rest." "No!" She cries, "You must go to the opera *now*!" "Now?!" "Now!" I say, "It's four o'clock in the morning." "Now!" she says. So I get up, get dressed, and drive over to the opera.

Bassene stands up and pulls his keychain out of his pocket. He firmly grasps a distinctively marked brass key.

BASSENE
I have my own key for just these special occasions. They didn't want to give it

to me. It was against policy. "You can't
go into the opera anytime you want!"
they said. "We have security guards
with schedules!" Well my muse has no
schedules. *She* comes to me anytime.
Night or day. I must be ready to serve,
so either make me a special key or get
someone else to direct your *Tosca*!

He laughs, defiantly dangling the key in front of CHRISTE's nose.

CUT TO

BINOCULAR POV OF JULIO BASSENE

PRINCE CHARMING studies the key. The binocular POV pans back to BASSENE's mouth.

PRINCE CHARMING
(*reading Bassene lips*)
"Isn't it beautiful? The brass was my idea.
It makes it so easy to see in the dark."

CUT TO

INT. BASSENE'S APARTMENT – NIGHT.

BASSENE
So last night I go back to the opera.
I walk onto the stage. There's the set for
the final scene. I sit in the first row and
imagine the singers onstage. Spoletta, the
sergeant, has assembled the firing squad.
The sky slowly brightens, it's almost
dawn. Spoletta approaches Cavaradossi,
Tosca's lover, to blindfold him, but he
refuses, pushing him away. And there,
huddled on the floor, is Tosca!
(*singing Tosca's part*)

"How long this delay is! What are they still waiting for? The sun's up already... I know it's only play-acting... but the suspense seems endless!"

(*narrating the action*)
Spoletta gives the firing squad their orders. They slowly raise their rifles and aim them at defiant Cavaradossi. He stands directly across the stage from them on the right.

(*jumping to feet shaking his head*)
"Wrong! Wrong! Wrong!" my muse screamed. "What's wrong?" I said. And then I saw it.

Bassene suddenly stops mid-sentence. He stares at CHRISTE's CAMERA CREW, like he's seeing them for the first time.

BASSENE
Who are these people?

CHRISTE
It's my crew.

BASSENE
Get them out of here. I can't spill my soul to strangers!

CHRISTE
But I need them for the interview.

BASSENE
Do you realize what I'm telling you? My most intimate secrets! Things I've never told any living being! And you want the world to hear them. How can you be so... brutally insensitive! There will be no interview!

And with a dramatic flourish, Bassene storms off into the bedroom, slamming the door behind him.

CHRISTE turns to her CAMERA CREW, slowly shaking her head.

>   CHRISTE
> I knew he was going to pull this.

She opens her bag and pulls out a cellular phone.

>   CHRISTE
> Jose, I want you and Luis to go
> downstairs and wait. In twenty minutes
> and not one second later I want you to
> call me on the cellular. The number is…

                                                    CUT TO

BINOCULAR POV OF CHRISTE MOUTHING THE NUMBERS.

>   PRINCE CHARMING
>   (*reading Christe's lips*)
>   402-1895

                                                    CUT TO

CHRISTE looking at her crew.

>   CHRISTE
> Now get going.

The CAMERA CREW leaves by the foyer door. CHRISTE puts the cellular phone back in her bag. She throws the bag over her shoulder and turns to face the closed bedroom door.

CHRISTE takes a deep breath and crosses over to it. She knocks. There's no response. She knocks again. Still nothing. She calls out.

CHRISTE
Mr. Bassene?

Still no answer. She slowly opens the door.

BASSENE is sitting on the bed with his back to CHRISTE. He stares out the darkened bedroom window.

CHRISTE takes a long look at the petulant fat spider perched in his web. How is she going to get her ass out of this one?

CHRISTE
Mr. Bassene? Are you all right?

BASSENE
(*whimpering*)
Yes. It's just the enormity of it all.

CHRISTE
(*not hearing a word he's saying*)
Excuse me?

BASSENE
(*even quieter*)
The horrendous enormity. But how could you understand?

CHRISTE
I'm sorry. I can't hear you.

BASSENE
(*quieter still*)
It doesn't matter.

CHRISTE crosses over to bed. She's closer now but still out of his reach.

CHRISTE
Please tell me what you saw.

BASSENE

Come closer.

CHRISTE walks around the bed and stands in front of BASSENE.

BASSENE

I saw that the firing squad was shooting in the wrong direction. The firing squad is stage right, Cavaradossi is stage left, Tosca's downstage center. What a feeble concept! Why not put Cavaradossi on the apron of the stage with his back to the audience? Put the firing squad stage center, then when they shoot, the audience will scream in terror because the guns are shooting right at them!

CHRISTE

What a fantastic idea!

BASSENE

Yes!
(pulling Christe into his arms)
I knew you'd understand.

CHRISTE

Please, Mr. Bassene!

CHRISTE tries to fight him off, but BASSENE is strong and wrestles her onto the bed.

BASSENE

You're so beautiful, I can't stop myself. Don't try and fight it. Our passion cannot be denied!

CHRISTE
(trying to push him off)
Please Mr. Bassene, we can't do this.

A muffled phone ring.

This distracts BASSENE long enough for CHRISTE to spring out of his grasp.

She backs away from the bed, fumbling to get the cellular phone out of her bag.

>   CHRISTE
>   (*breathless*)
> It's the office. They only call when
> something's urgent.

BASSENE's body sags with frustration. The fly has escaped. CHRISTE hits the send button and puts the phone to her ear.

Extreme close-up of phone pressed to CHRISTE's ear.

>   PRINCE CHARMING
> Ambrose Chapel.

CHRISTE's head jerks.

Sleeping Beauty has just been kissed.

She awakes and waits for instructions.

>   PRINCE CHARMING
> Get the brass key from his keychain. Slip
> it under the hallway door.

CHRISTE returns the cellular phone back to her bag.

She drops the bag to the floor.

She walks around the bed and faces BASSENE. He looks up at her. A confused expression on his face.

CHRISTE unbuttons her blouse and lets it drop to the floor. She unzips her skirt and steps out of it. Never taking her eyes off of BASSENE.

She unhooks her bra and takes off her panties. She stands naked before him. He's stunned by his good fortune.

                 CHRISTE
          (*sultry like we've never seen her*)
     Get those clothes off. I want to see you
     naked.

BASSENE springs into action, tearing off his clothes until he's as naked as she is.

                 CHRISTE
     Lie down on your back and close your
     eyes.

Like a trained dog, BASSENE flips over on his back and closes his eyes.

CHRISTE reaches down, picks up his pants, pulls out his keychain.

                 BASSENE
     What's that?

                 CHRISTE
     Shut up. You'll know soon enough.

CHRISTE slips the brass key off the key ring and returns the chain to the pocket of BASSENE's pants.

                 CHRISTE
     Where's the record player?

                 BASSENE
     In the living room.

                    CHRISTE
I'm going to put on some special music. If
you open your eyes before my return,
I will be gone forever. Do you understand
me?

                    BASSENE
Yes.

                    CHRISTE
One little peek.
        (*she lightly brushes his penis*)
And you will never see me again.

                    BASSENE
Yes. I understand.

CHRISTE silently picks up her bag and her clothes and leaves the bedroom.

She crosses the living room to the foyer, kneels down and slips the brass key under the door and out onto the hallway carpet.

Now that CHRISTE has completed her instructions, her head jerks and she wakes up.

Naked, kneeling on the floor in front of the apartment door. Christe springs to her feet. Shocked at what's happened to her.

She has no memory of anything after she heard "Ambrose Chapel" on her cellular phone. She frantically pulls her clothes on.

The cellular phone rings.

CHRISTE looks at the bag on the floor, afraid to open it.

The phone rings again.

She finally reaches down and opens her bag.

The phone rings again.

She takes out the phone. Presses it to her ear.

The phone rings again.

CHRISTE pushes the send button.

> JOSE
> Hey, Christe. It's Jose. Has the spider pounced yet?

CUT TO

THE SPIDER, still on his back.

Eyes closed.

Forever obedient.

INT. APARTMENT HALLWAY – NIGHT.

The brass key is lying on the carpet.

A hand reaches down and picks it up.

INT. WOLFE'S HOTEL ROOM – DAY.

CHRISTE sits in a chair facing WOLFE. She's been talking non-stop. WOLFE is trying to take notes but he can't keep up with CHRISTE's rapid-fire delivery. Finally, he interrupts.

> WOLFE
> Slow down. Slow down. I can't get this all down if you speak so fast.

CHRISTE
I'm sorry. Just so much has happened.

WOLFE
Let's go back to your mother first.
(*referring to his notes*)
She says your father may have done things to you. But you say you have absolutely no memory of anything like that happening?

CHRISTE
I don't know what he was doing but it wasn't abuse.

WOLFE
But why would she say that?

CHRISTE
I don't know.

WOLFE
I think the key here is, you have no memory of anything happening. Just like you have no memory of taking your clothes off in Bassene's apartment.
(*looks down at his notes again*)
In your dream you remember your father saying, "If you say anything to anybody, your child will die!" What's important here is not the instructions. But who's giving the instructions.

CHRISTE
My father.

WOLFE
The same father that you thought you saw in the park.

CHRISTE
But I must have been mistaken.

WOLFE
But even if you thought you saw him, that would trigger the dream. And there's something about this dream that isn't a dream. Why would I remember the cymbals? I thought about it. I don't remember having a dream with cymbals in it. It's from something else. Like Hypnotic Programming. I talked to a friend of mine here at the convention. He's an expert in the field. When I told him about your case he was sure you were a Sleeping Beauty.

CHRISTE
A what?

WOLFE
A Sleeping Beauty. Someone that has been programmed to do something that their conscious mind is totally unaware of. They are awakened with a password, it's called a "kiss," and given instructions. Once the instructions are carried out, they return to their normal conscious state with no memory of what happened. What was the last thing you remember before you woke up in Bassene's living room?

CHRISTE
I got a phone call.

WOLFE
From who?

CHRISTE
I don't remember.

WOLFE
Was it your father?

CHRISTE
How could it be?

WOLFE
Christe, your father had some type of psychological training. He worked for some secret government organization in Virginia. This organization developed mind-control programs that he may have used on you when you were a child. Now you're having dreams about shooting somebody or witnessing an assassination. Could your father be using you again?

CHRISTE
Are you telling me my father is some kind of mad Dr. Frankenstein? That's ridiculous. Anyway, he's dead.

WOLFE
Did anyone ever identify his body?

CHRISTE
No, it was destroyed in the explosion.

WOLFE
But he turned up in the park.

CHRISTE
I must have been mistaken.

WOLFE
Maybe not. How would he know to call you at Bassene's?

CHRISTE
(*sarcastic*)
He followed me. Isn't that what ghosts do?

WOLFE
What were you doing there?

CHRISTE
(*exasperated*)
Trying to interview a horny opera director!

WOLFE
Doesn't your dream take place at an opera?

CHRISTE
No. It's a concert hall.

WOLFE
What is Mr. Bassene directing?

CHRISTE
Tosca. It opens tomorrow. It's Bassene's big night because the president of the...
(*suddenly Christe gets it*)
Is that who's going to be assassinated?!

WOLFE
It's a possibility.

CHRISTE
Someone is going to assassinate the president?
(*shaking her head*)
C'mon! You can't prove any of this.

WOLFE
What happens if you get another call?

CHRISTE
I guess, like a good robot, I'll do what I'm instructed.

WOLFE
And if that includes shooting the president?

CHRISTE
That's ludicrous. I've never even fired a gun.

WOLFE
That you remember.

CHRISTE
I would remember that!

WOLFE
Did you remember taking your clothes off?

CHRISTE
(*sarcastic*)
Okay. So maybe I took shooting lessons under hypnosis. I'm sick of all this, and you too, Doctor. None of what you say makes any sense to me. So why don't we just call it quits?

CHRISTE gets up to leave.

WOLFE
Wait a minute. Will you give me a chance to convince you?

CHRISTE
How?

WOLFE
I want to video record Sleeping Beauty.

CHRISTE
How do you plan to do that?

WOLFE
When do you interview Bassene?

CHRISTE
Backstage. After the performance.

WOLFE
Do you mind if I'm there with my camcorder?

CHRISTE
No, why?

WOLFE
If you get any calls, I'll get it on tape. I'm sure it will be quite convincing when I play it back to you. It's a technique we use for multiple personality patients.

CHRISTE
Dr. Jekyll gets to see video of Mr. Hyde??

WOLFE
Something like that.

CHRISTE
Okay. But you must promise me something.

WOLFE
Yes.

CHRISTE
If I pull out a gun, and start blasting away, you'll put down your camera and stop me.

WOLFE
Of course.

CHRISTE
Thanks.
(gets up to leave)
Call me tomorrow. I'll be...

WOLFE
(interrupting)
Christe, I'm going to be by your side from now on. You could be "kissed" anytime.

CHRISTE
Only by you, doctor. What would you like for dinner?

WOLFE
One other thing. This meeting ends our formal doctor-to-patient relationship. I can't treat you anymore.

CHRISTE
One kiss joke and it's goodbye Christe?

WOLFE
I'm getting too involved with you. Very unprofessional. But I can't pretend it's not happening.

CHRISTE
(touching his hand)
It's happening to me too.

WOLFE
(gently pulling away)
Let's try to get through this thing without any more complications. When everything's back to normal, I call you up and make a date. Take you to the movies.

                    CHRISTE
            (*staring straight in his eyes*)
            Will there be any kissing?

                     WOLFE
                   (*smiling*)
            I don't know about kissing on the first
            date.
                (*trying to change the subject*)
            But, right now, I'm looking forward to
            meeting your mother.

                    CHRISTE
            Not tonight. She's staying with Ruben at
            her brother's house. My uncle's Chief of
            Police.

                     WOLFE
            Good idea. It will just take a second for
            me to throw a few things in a bag.

                    CHRISTE
            I'll wait downstairs, Dr. Wolfe.

                     WOLFE
            No. No. I'm just plain Nick now.

                                        DISSOLVE TO

INT. THE KITCHEN IN CHRISTE'S APARTMENT – NIGHT.

It's a little after nine. CHRISTE finishes loading the dirty dinner dishes in the dishwasher.

She walks out into the living room where WOLFE is checking out his camcorder.

                    CHRISTE
            Is everything working okay?

                    WOLFE
I think so. I'm just trying to get the time
and date set right.
    (*holding up the manual in his lap*)
You have to be a nuclear physicist to
figure these things out.

                   CHRISTE
I have to be up at five, so I'm going to bed.
I hope you'll be comfortable on the couch.

                    WOLFE
I'll be fine. Thanks a lot, and I'll see you
in the morning.

                   CHRISTE
Good night.

CHRISTE leaves the living room. WOLFE turns back to the camcorder.

INT. CHRISTE'S BEDROOM – NIGHT.

CHRISTE enters her bedroom. She takes off her clothes and pulls on a white nightgown.

She gets into bed, turns on a reading light, and picks up a book from the bedside table.

Suddenly the phone rings. CHRISTE reaches over to answer it.

                    WOLFE
          (*yelling from the other room*)
              DON'T PICK IT UP!

CHRISTE freezes.

She looks at the telephone.

It rings again. She looks at her watch.

CHRISTE
(*yelling back*)
It's Ruben, he always calls before he goes to bed.

WOLFE
Just wait one second, I'll be right there.

CHRISTE folds her arms and waits. The phone rings again.

CHRISTE
He'll be very upset if I don't answer.

WOLFE comes through the door holding the camcorder. He zooms into CHRISTE's face.

WOLFE
Okay. I'm ready. Answer it.

CHRISTE picks up the phone.

CHRISTE
Hi Mom. Just a few more days, I promise. So don't go in the living room. Okay, put him on… Hi honey… I was just reading. Yes, that's right, Grandma did call Mommy on the phone. Did you have a nice dinner?
(*cupping her hand over the phone*)
It's Ruben.

WOLFE drops the CAMCORDER from his eye. He smiles and leaves the room.

CHRISTE
(*taking her hand away from the phone*)
No, honey, you can't play with Anna's figurines. They're not toys. I can't go tomorrow. Mommy's got to work.

INT. LIVING ROOM – NIGHT.

WOLFE walks in, puts the camcorder down on the table. It's pointed toward the television set, still recording.

WOLFE sits back down on the couch, landing right on top of the remote control. The television switches on at full volume.

INT. CHRISTE BEDROOM – NIGHT.

CHRISTE jumps. The television is blaring from the living room.

> CHRISTE
> (*to her son on the phone*)
> Look, honey, there's something wrong
> with the TV. I'll call you right back.

CHRISTE hangs up the phone, gets out of bed and walks into the living room.

> CUT TO

INT. LIVING ROOM – NIGHT.

On the television screen is Hitchcock's *The Man Who Knew Too Much*. When CHRISTE enters the room, JIMMY STEWART is speaking.

> JIMMY STEWART
> AMBROSE CHAPEL! It's not a person,
> it's a place!

CHRISTE jerks.

She's just been kissed.

                    WOLFE
            (*hardly audible over the
            earsplitting television set*)
        I'm sorry. I sat on it.
            (*fumbling with the remote control*)
        Does this turn it off?

WOLFE is turned toward the television set. His back is to CHRISTE.

The button he's pushed just changes the channel. It's another movie: *Walk on the Wild Side*. It's the credit sequence, a tracking shot of a black cat walking through a garbage-littered street.

The soundtrack is an ear-splitting song carrying one simple command: "TAKE A WALK ON THE WILD SIDE! I SAID TAKE A WALK ON THE WILD SIDE!"

CHRISTE's head jerks again.

She's gotten her instructions.

She turns around and walks out the door.

WOLFE doesn't see CHRISTE leave. He's too occupied with hitting buttons on the remote control.

The television switches back to *The Man Who Knew Too Much*. Finally, he hits the mute button and the television goes silent.

He turns back to face CHRISTE. She's not there.

                    WOLFE
        Christe?

He walks toward the bedroom.

INT. CHRISTE'S BEDROOM – NIGHT.

WOLFE enters. She's not there. He crosses the room to the closed door leading to the bathroom. He knocks on it.

                    WOLFE
Christe?

No answer. He pushes the door open and looks inside. She's not there. He turns around and leaves the bedroom.

INT. KITCHEN – NIGHT.

WOLFE walks into the kitchen. Still no CHRISTE.

INT. HALLWAY – NIGHT.

WOLFE comes into the hallway from the kitchen. He walks down to the room at the end. He pushes open the door.

INT. RUBEN'S ROOM – NIGHT.

WOLFE looks inside. No sign of CHRISTE. He closes the door.

EXT. APARTMENT BUILDING – NIGHT.

WOLFE walks out of the building and looks up and down the street.

Still no CHRISTE.

He walks back into the building.

INT. LIVING ROOM – NIGHT.

WOLFE enters the room and sits down on the couch.

He doesn't know what to think and has no idea where CHRISTE's gone.

He looks up at the television set where *The Man Who Knew Too Much* is still playing. There's a blonde woman, JO (played by DORIS DAY), standing in the concert hall. From her viewpoint she sees the complete hall and the orchestra playing up onstage.

The camera moves into the back of the stage where a TALL DISTINGUISHED MAN in a tuxedo sits next to a chair. On the chair rests a large pair of cymbals.

CUT TO

Extreme close-up of WOLFE's face.

> WOLFE
> (*realizing this movie is Christe's dream*)
> Jesus!

CUT TO

EXT. THE WILD SIDE – NIGHT.

The most dangerous street in Mexico City. Peopled with hookers, pimps, drug dealers, beggars, punks, thugs. The absolute dregs of the city.

Walking down this street, barefoot and in her white nightgown, is CHRISTE.

The people she walks by stare after her in shocked disbelief. Is this some crazy woman on a suicide stroll?

She passes THREE BURLY THUGS. They exchange leering looks and take off after her.

CUT TO

A dark alley.

CHRISTE crosses the street leading into the alley.

The THREE THUGS come up behind her and drag her into it.

One clamps his forearm around her throat and backs her up against a brick wall.

The other two stand in front of her.

THUG ONE pulls out a gun and points it right between her eyes.

>THUG ONE
>You see this honey? It's gonna give you a third eye.

CHRISTE, completely emotionless, stares back at him.

>THUG ONE
>Now you listen to me, and listen to me good. Who told you you could pedal your pretty ass down here?

>CHRISTE
>(*emotionless*)
>I was taking a walk.

>THUG TWO
>(*mocking her*)
>Taking a walk?

>CHRISTE
>(*dead serious*)
>That's right, taking a walk.

>THUG ONE
>Don't you know you just don't "walk" down here.

CHRISTE
Why not?

THUG ONE
Because this is my block!

CHRISTE
Why?

THUG ONE
Because I say it is!

CHRISTE
That doesn't make any sense.

THUG THREE
Let's just fuck the bitch!

CHRISTE
(*unafraid*)
Would you please get out of my way.
I have to finish my walk.

THUG ONE
(*can't believe the nerve of this girl*)
You have to do what?

CHRISTE
(*firmly*)
To finish my walk.

THUG ONE
Am I in your way?

CHRISTE
Yes.

THUG ONE
Excuse me.

THUG ONE backs away a few steps.

> THUG ONE
> Give the girl some space.

THUG TWO takes a step backwards.

> CHRISTE
> *(to Thug Three,*
> *who holds her from behind)*
> Let me go. I have to finish my walk.

> THUG ONE
> *(to Thug Three)*
> You heard the lady? Let her go.

THUG THREE slowly relaxes his grip.

> CHRISTE
> Thank you.

> THUG ONE
> *(cocking the gun)*
> Now down on your knees, bitch, and
> show us how good you suck.

Christe jolts into action.

She brings her knee up hard into THUG ONE's groin.

He doubles over, gasping in pain.

The gun drops from his hand, but before it hits the ground, Christe grabs it.

She whirls around, delivering a roundhouse kick to the jaw of THUG THREE

His head smashes into the brick wall.

THUG TWO, knife drawn, lunges at Christe's back.

Christe turns towards him. She raises the gun and fires at him point blank.

> CUT TO

INT. CHRISTE'S LIVING ROOM – NIGHT.

WOLFE is on the phone. He has the camcorder in his hand. He's hooked up to the television and he's playing it back.

On the television is a shot of the television from over CHRISTE's shoulder.

She has just entered the room.

JIMMY STEWART is saying "Ambrose Chapel."

CHRISTE jerks.

WOLFE hits the still button and the frame freezes.

> WOLFE
> (*into the phone*)
> I'm sure the kiss is "Ambrose Chapel."

> MONTANA
> (*on the phone*)
> What happened then?

> WOLFE
> She disappeared.

> MONTANA
> (on the phone)
> What's the next thing she heard after "Ambrose Chapel"?

                    WOLFE
Let me look.

WOLFE hits the play button.

The television channel changes to *Walk on the Wild Side*. The sound is distorted but deafeningly clear.

CHRISTE'S shoulders jerk.

She turns around and walks out of the camcorder frame.

WOLFE hit the still button.

The frame freezes.

                    WOLFE
Take a walk on the wild side.

                    MONTANA
                (over the phone)
I heard it.

                    WOLFE
What does it mean?

                    MONTANA
                (over the phone)
She took a walk.

                    WOLFE
Where?

                    MONTANA
                (over the phone)
On the wild side. Wherever the hell that is.

                    WOLFE
What should I do?

MONTANA
(*over the phone*)
Nothing. She'll come back after the walk.

WOLFE
(*concerned*)
She was in her nightgown.

MONTANA
(*over the phone*)
There's nothing you can do about it now. How long has she been gone?

WOLFE
(*looking at his watch*)
Over an hour. Shouldn't I call the police?

MONTANA
(*over the phone*)
Give her another hour. I'm sure she'll come back.

WOLFE
Okay. So I watched it to the end. It's her dream.

MONTANA
(*over the phone*)
Damn smart idea.

WOLFE
How do you mean?

MONTANA
(*over the phone*)
When you program a Sleeping Beauty, years in advance, you have to give them a good cover memory in case they fall into enemy hands. A story that's like

what they're programmed to do. Then if they get captured and someone starts poking around in their heads, all they come up with is the cover memory, which looks sinister enough, but of course is all make-believe. But using a movie is really ingenious, you don't have to give them a verbal scenario, you just sit them down, dope them up, and feed it right into their subconscious. Movies are constructed to make you identify with the characters anyway. In Christe's case, they just told her she *was* the character.

> WOLFE
> So what do I do now?

> MONTANA
> (*on the phone*)
> Just watch her. She's going to go into action at the opera tomorrow and you'll see what's she's programmed to do. If she starts to do anything dangerous just say "Ambrose Chapel." That will stop her dead.

The doorbell rings.

> WOLFE
> It's the doorbell.

> MONTANA
> (*over the phone*)
> That's probably her. I'll see you tomorrow.

> WOLFE
> Tomorrow?

                    MONTANA
                  (*over the phone*)
            Didn't you know I was an opera lover?
            And I wouldn't miss this *Tosca* for the
            world.

WOLFE hangs up the phone and goes to the door.

He opens it. In the doorway stands CHRISTE. Her white nightgown is covered with blood. Her anguished face stares up into WOLFE's eyes.

                    CHRISTE
            What's happening to me?

EXT. TEXAS SKY – DAY.

A large private jet streaks across the sky.

                                                CUT TO

INT. JET – DAY.

MAJOR, SPECTOR and KEEN sit around a table. Drinks, chips, cards and snacks are spread out before them. They're playing blackjack.

                    MAJOR
            This is the craziest idea you ever had.

                    SPECTOR
            That's how you win elections: hit them
            with the unexpected. When Carvel got
            Clinton to play his sax on *The Tonight
            Show*, now that was genius!

                    MAJOR
            Well this ain't no *Tonight Show*. These
            Mexicans hate me. Hit me!

KEEN deals MAJOR a card. It's an Ace.

KEEN
That's why you have to be there. To show you're not a hard loser. You've got to press the flesh, mend a few fences.

MAJOR
Shit I do. When I'm president the first thing I'm going to do is build a border wall thirty feet high. Hit me again!

KEEN
But you're not president yet.

MAJOR
Judging by today's poll, I'm never going to be. C'mon, I said, hit me.

KEEN puts the deck down. He reaches below the table for his briefcase. He opens it and hands MAJOR a handwritten speech.

KEEN
Take this with you tonight.

MAJOR
What is it?

KEEN
It's your "Out of tragedy comes a new beginning" speech.

MAJOR
Sounds a little depressing.

KEEN
It will be historic.

                    MAJOR
          But why tonight?

                    SPECTOR
          Your time has come.

                    MAJOR
          It has?

EXT. SUBURBAN HOUSE OF CHRISTE'S UNCLE, MIGUEL SERRANO – DUSK

PRINCE CHARMING, dressed as a METRO POLICEMAN, walks up to the front door and rings the doorbell.

After a few seconds ANNA SERRANO opens it. She's a tank of a women with a perpetually sour expression on her face. She's buttoning up her coat.

                    ANNA
          Yes.

                    PRINCE CHARMING
          Is Ruben Rivera here?

                    ANNA
          He certainly is. But you're not coming in
          here like that.

                    PRINCE CHARMING
          Excuse me?

                    ANNA
          Would you please wipe that dirt off your
          feet?
                    (*calling upstairs*)
          Miguel, it's one of your boys for Ruben.

PRINCE CHARMING carefully wipes the dirt off his feet on the doormat. ANNA stares down at his shoes with a critical eye.

> ANNA
> You better just take them off.

PRINCE CHARMING starts taking off his shoes.

> ANNA
> Do you know what that brat did yesterday?

> PRINCE CHARMING
> No, ma'am.

> ANNA
> He took my favorite porcelain giraffe off the mantelpiece! The way they raise children today is a crime.

> PRINCE CHARMING
> Yes, ma'am.

> ANNA
> And it was a miracle it wasn't in a million pieces all over my white carpet!

> PRINCE CHARMING
> Yes, ma'am.

> ANNA
> You'll have to talk to my husband. I'm late.
> *(looking down at his socks)*
> And stay out here. I don't like the look of those socks.

ANNA dashes past him. PRINCE CHARMING watches her disappear down the street. He slips his shoes back on.

He turns around to face a massive man in his late fifties. This is MIGUEL SARRANO. He's dressed in a light-colored business suit and he's eyeing PRINCE CHARMING with suspicion.

> MIGUEL SERRANO
> Yes?

> PRINCE CHARMING
> Is Ruben Rivera here?

> MIGUEL SERRANO
> (*looking at Prince Charming's uniform*)
> Who are you?

> PRINCE CHARMING
> City police. There's been an accident.

> MIGUEL SERRANO
> No kidding.
> (*pulling out his service revolver
> and pointing it at Prince Charming*)
> Why don't you come in and tell me about it?

> PRINCE CHARMING
> What are you doing?

> MIGUEL SERRANO
> Just get your hands up and turn around.

PRINCE CHARMING raises his hands. MIGUEL pats him down.

> MIGUEL SERRANO
> (*standing up behind him*)
> Now drop your gun belt!

PRINCE CHARMING slowly unbuckles his gun belt. Gripping it tightly, he suddenly whips it around, knocking the gun out of MIGUEL'S HAND.

It falls to the floor. As MIGUEL lunges for it, PRINCE CHARMING smashes him in the jaw.

MIGUEL falls back through the doorway onto the immaculate white rug covering the floor of ANNA SERRANO'S PERFECT LIVING ROOM.

On every table, mantelpiece, window ledge, every inch of flat space in the room, is a delicate porcelain animal.

MIGUEL jumps to his feet and he and PRINCE CHARMING start to fight. They're both big men and equally matched in combat skills. It's violent, brutal, and dirty.

They punch, kick, scratch, bite until they, and everything else is wrecked.

Not one figurine survives.

And neither does MIGUEL, who finally gets caught in the vise-like grip of PRINCE CHARMING's forearms. The life is literally squeezed out of him.

PRINCE CHARMING slowly stands up, dusting shattered glass off his chest and arms.

>   RUBEN
>   (*calling from upstairs*)
> Uncle Miguel? Did Grandma get the ice cream?

PRINCE CHARMING turns toward the staircase leading upstairs.

RUBEN comes bounding down.

He stops at the sight of the trashed living room and his GREAT-UNCLE stretched out in the middle of the floor.

                    RUBEN
               (*looking at Prince Charming*)
          He fell down.

                PRINCE CHARMING
          That's right, son.

RUBEN moves off the staircase and over to his prone GREAT-UNCLE. He kneels down next to his head.

                    RUBEN
          Uncle Miguel?

PRINCE CHARMING moves around behind the boy.

Suddenly he loops his forearm around RUBEN's throat, clamping down on his windpipe.

The boy gasps for breath, struggling to free himself from his attacker. But it's all over in a few seconds.

PRINCE CHARMING gently places the unconscious boy down next to SERRANO. He reaches into his pocket and takes out a small case.

He pops it open and removes a syringe, a bottle of alcohol, and a cotton ball. He carefully sterilizes the syringe needle.

The phone rings. PRINCE CHARMING doesn't even react. He takes a small bottle of clear liquid out of his pocket and plunges the syringe into it

INT. CHRISTE'S OFFICE – DAY.

CHRISTE is on the phone. After three more rings she hangs up. She turns to WOLFE, who is sitting across the desk from her.

CHRISTE
Still no answer. Where can they be?

WOLFE
She said they were going home tonight?

CHRISTE
Yes. Mom said she was going to start dinner at five. Something's wrong. I'm going over there.

WOLFE
Maybe they all went out for a hamburger or something.

CHRISTE's producer, RAMON, walks into the office.

RAMON
I don't know what you did to Mr. Bassene but he's refusing to talk to you or anyone else from this station. You better get over there and straighten this out.

CHRISTE
I can't go now.

RAMON
Why not?

CHRISTE
I'm worried about my son.

RAMON
(*blowing up*)
Jesus, Christe, I don't have any time for your family problems. You fucked up the Bassene interview and now we can't cover one of the most important events this city's ever had. Now get over there

and make nice to that asshole so we can
get our cameras in there tonight, or get
yourself another job.

The PRODUCER slams out of CHRISTE's office.

                CHRISTE
I've got to do something! I have this
terrible feeling Ruben's been kidnapped.

                WOLFE
Just think for a second. You know that's
the dream. And you know it isn't real. It's
just a movie.

The phone rings. CHRISTE picks it up.

                          CUT TO

Tight close-up of CHRISTE's face as she puts the receiver to hear ear. Her face goes white as she listens.

WOLFE picks up the camcorder, points it at CHRISTE, and presses record.

CHRISTE slowly put the phone down.

                WOLFE
Who was it?

                CHRISTE
My father.

                WOLFE
Your father! What did he say?

                CHRISTE
Go to the opera.

                    WOLFE
Is that all?

                    CHRISTE
No.
    (*her face filling with fear*)
"If you say anything to anybody, your
child will die!"

                                            CUT TO

EXT. REAR OF PALACIO DE BELLAS ARTES (THE OPERA HOUSE) – EARLY EVENING.

PRINCE CHARMING, still dressed as a METRO POLICEMAN, walks to the far right exit door. He is carrying a long cylindrical package. Using BASSENE's brass key, he unlocks the door and goes inside.

INT. BACKSTAGE – EARLY EVENING.

PRINCE CHARMING wanders through the backstage pre-opening opera chaos. He finally stops outside of an open dressing room door.

INT. DRESSING ROOM – EARLY EVENING.

Inside are a group of ten actors getting into their SOLDIER COSTUMES. Some are trying on grotesque skull masks.

Right inside the doorway is a barrel filled with PROP RIFLES.

Finally, one of the actors, dressed and masked, walks out of the dressing room.

INT. HALLWAY OUTSIDE OF DRESSING ROOM – EARLY EVENING.

The ACTOR walks down the hallway. PRINCE CHARMING follows.

INT. STAIRCASE OFF HALLWAY – EARLY EVENING.

The ACTOR emerges from the hallway and down the staircase. PRINCE CHARMING follows a few steps behind.

INT. HALLWAY AT FOOT OF STAIRCASE – EARLY EVENING.

The ACTOR comes off the staircase and walks toward the MEN'S ROOM at the end of the hallway. PRINCE CHARMING stops at the foot of the stairs and looks up and down the hallway. It is deserted.

INT. MEN'S ROOM – EARLY EVENING.

The ACTOR enters. It's a large room with a long row of ten sinks facing one wall and toilet stalls against the other.

There are THREE MEN washing their hands. The ACTOR crosses the room and heads for the stall at the far end of the room.

A moment later, PRINCE CHARMING enters the room. He watches as the ACTOR goes in the last stall and closes the door behind him.

PRINCE CHARMING walks down the line of sinks, stopping in front of the one directly opposite the stall the ACTOR entered.

He rests his long package against the wall and starts to wash his hands. In the mirror above the sink, he can see a reflection of the stalls.

PRINCE CHARMING turns to his right and watches the THREE MEN finish drying their hands and go out the door.

PRINCE CHARMING turns around and slowly moves toward the only occupied stall.

EXT. AIRPORT – EARLY EVENING.

MAJOR's PLANE sits on the tarmac. Beside it is a long limousine.

MAJOR, SPECTOR and KEEN emerge from the plane dressed in tuxedoes. A CHAUFFEUR holds the door of the limo open. MAJOR, SPECTOR and KEEN walk down the ramp toward it.

> MAJOR
> Are you sure you're telling me everything?

> KEEN
> Of course not. I'm your Mister Deniability.

> MAJOR
> You're not doing anything that's going to embarrass me?

> KEEN
> I'm guaranteeing your election and the future of our country. That's all that matters.

> MAJOR
> If you two are pulling some kind of dirty trick, I want to know about it.

> SPECTOR
> What dirty trick?

MAJOR
I don't know.

KEEN
That's all you have to remember. YOU DON'T KNOW! Every possible link to you is being eliminated. But, of course, to be a hundred per cent safe, you'll have to sacrifice us.

MAJOR
(*a wry smile*)
That's not a problem for me. Is it a problem for you?

KEEN
(*smiling back*)
No, sir!

SPECTOR
No, sir!

MAJOR
Good. Let's get on to the show.

EXT. CITY STREET – NIGHT.

A TV van moves slowly through the city traffic.

INT. TV VAN – NIGHT.

WOLFE and CHRISTE sit in the back. The two-man VIDEO CREW sits up front with the driver.

CHRISTE
You've got to find Ruben. My uncle's house is not far from the opera.

WOLFE
I can't leave you. Suppose your father calls again.

CHRISTE
To give me more orders? To do what? Shoot the ambassador? The president? Tosca? I don't give a damn!
(opening her bag and taking out a pen)
It's off Hidalgo Avenue.
(writing down an address and a telephone number on a piece of paper)
This is my uncle's address and my phone number. As soon as you find anything, call me.

WOLFE
(taking the paper)
Okay.

CHRISTE
(calling to the driver)
Juan, pull over here.

JUAN
I was told to make no stops.

CHRISTE
Pull over or I'm getting out right now.

JUAN
Okay, but Mr. Ramon said…

CHRISTE
Just do what I say!

EXT. CITY STREET – NIGHT.

The VAN pulls over to the side of the road. The door slides open and WOLFE hops out.

EXT. PALACIO DE BELLAS ARTES (MEXICAN CITY OPERA HOUSE) – NIGHT.

A long line of limousines drop off various dignitaries at the entrance to the opera house.

There's a huge security force circling the whole building. They are checking everyone's tickets and holding back the PUBLIC and the PRESS from the arriving patrons.

THE PRESIDENT OF MEXICO arrives, escorting THE PRESIDENT OF THE UNITED STATES.

They are surrounded by a court of acolytes and an army of bodyguards. They stop for a moment before the PHOTOGRAPHERS and PRESS, wave and smile, and quickly move on into the theatre.

INT. OPERA BACKSTAGE MEN'S ROOM – NIGHT.

A WORM'S EYE VIEW OF THE LAST STALL.

There are a pair of naked feet resting on the floor next to the base of the toilet bowl.

Moving closer and craning up and over the locked stall door we discover the ACTOR, unconscious and stripped, seated on the toilet.

Panning over to the next stall we see PRINCE CHARMING, dressed in the ACTOR'S SOLDIER COSTUME, reading a newspaper. His skull mask is pushed away from his face and rests on the top of his head. Next to him is the contents of the long cylindrical package.

It leans against the tile wall directly behind him. It's a turn-of-the-century Roman military rifle.

Identical to the prop ones sitting in the barrel we saw in the dressing room.

EXT. OPERA – NIGHT.

MAJOR gets out of his limousine and walks toward the entrance. KEEN and SPECTOR are a few steps behind. MAJOR is called over to the CORDONED-OFF PRESS.

> WOMEN REPORTER
> Major Bacon! Major Bacon! Why are you here tonight?

> MAJOR
> (*mischievous smile*)
> Didn't you know I was a great opera lover?

> MALE REPORTER
> Isn't this pretty far to go for *Tosca*?

> WOMEN REPORTER
> Does the president know you're here?

> MAJOR
> (*all innocence*)
> Is *he* here tonight? Gosh, is that a coincidence. I didn't know he liked opera.

> MALE REPORTER
> Aren't you a little uncomfortable here after all the critical things you said about the Mexican people?

> MAJOR
> (*deeply offended*)
> I love the Mexican people. They're a noble, beautiful, hard-working folk.

What I was talking about was those rich
businessmen down here that are cheating
their own workers out of a fair wage
and driving them across the border to
take jobs from good Americans. I love
America, and I love this country too.

                WOMEN REPORTER
When are you going to announce your
candidacy?

                MAJOR
Only if the people want me.

                MALE REPORTER
Are you going to meet with the president?

                MAJOR
                (*backing away*)
Hey, folks. I have to go. I don't want to
miss the beginning.

INT. BASSENE'S BACKSTAGE OFFICE – NIGHT.

CHRISTE'S CREW waits outside.

The door swings open and a smiling Bassene swaggers out
and crosses over to the stage.

CHRISTE is a few steps behind him. She walks over to the
CREW.

                CHRISTE
Everything's fine. Let's get some shots of
him in the wings during the opera.

                JOSE
What did you do?

                    CHRISTE
          Promised him my ass, among other
          things. Let's go.

EXT. THE SERRANO SUBURBAN HOUSE – DAY.

A TAXI pulls up and WOLFE gets out. He walks up to the front door and rings the bell.

There's no answer. He moves across the porch and looks in the window.

WOLFE's POV through the window.

The living room. No sign of RUBEN or CHRISTE's UNCLE.

WOLFE walks around to the side of the house and looks in the kitchen window.

WOLFE's POV through the kitchen window. The kitchen. No one there, either.

WOLFE continues around the house to the backyard. He walks up the back porch steps and tries the back door.

It opens.

INT. KITCHEN – NIGHT.

WOLFE enters the kitchen and calls out.

                    WOLFE
          Ruben? Ruben!

There's no answer.

INT. STAGE OF THE OPERA – NIGHT.

The set is SCARPIA's room in the Farnese Palace. The table is laid for supper. Downstage center is a large window that opens on to the courtyard of the Palace. It's the end of the second act.

TOSCA is begging SCARPIA to save the life of her lover, CAVARADOSSI. SCARPIA is making a cruel bargain with her

> SCARPIA
> (*singing*)
> Do you hear? It's the drums approaching, escorting the condemned on their last journey. Time is passing! You know what grim preparations are being made down there? They're erecting a gallows. By your decision, a mere hour of life is left to your Mario.

TOSCA, overcome by grief, falls onto the settee. SCARPIA coldly continues to gaze at her.

> TOSCA
> (*singing*)
> I have lived for art, I have lived for love, and never harmed a living soul!

Panning off Tosca, over to the wings. There is Bassene watching the singers.

A few feet farther CHRISTE'S VIDEO CREW is shooting. Next to them is CHRISTE. She is paying little attention to Bassene or his opera and every few moments looks nervously at her watch.

Panning off CHRISTIE onto the audience and up into the boxes.

Zooming in on MAJOR BACON's box.

It's at the extreme left, adjacent to the proscenium, allowing the MAJOR, SPECTOR and KEEN to see into the wings, where CHRISTE stands next to her VIDEO CREW. The three of them seem to be enjoying the opera immensely.

There is a conspicuously empty fourth seat.

KEEN takes a look to his left. Panning off KEEN and up to the Presidential Box.

There sits the PRESIDENT OF MEXICO and the PRESIDENT OF THE UNITED STATES.

Between them, a few feet behind, is the MEXICAN AMBASSADOR.

Panning off the PRESIDENT OF THE UNITED STATES and down to the stage.

SCARPIA is impatient with TOSCA.

SCARPIA
(*singing*)
Make up your mind!

TOSCA
(*singing*)
Must I kneel and beg for pity? Look,
I implore you with clasped hands! See,
here I am, defeated, pleading for a single
word of mercy.

SCARPIA
(*singing*)
Tosca, you are too lovely and too
enchanting. I yield. The bargain is a poor
one: you ask of me a life, I ask of you but
a moment!

                    TOSCA
            (*rising, and singing with the
                utmost contempt*)
        Pah! You revolt me!

INT. SECOND FLOOR OF RIVERA'S HOUSE – NIGHT.

WOLFE walks down the hallway, opening each bedroom door and looking inside. There's no sign of RUBEN. Finally, he returns to the head of the staircase and goes down.

INT. DOWNSTAIRS FOYER – NIGHT.

WOLFE walks over to a small telephone table. Next to it is a door leading to the cellar.

He picks up the phone and puts it to his ear. It's dead. He reels the cord in and discovers it's been ripped out of the wall.

Now he knows there's been foul play.

WOLFE looks around again and notices the cellar door next to the telephone table. He reaches for the doorknob and twists it.

It's locked.

He tries to force the latch by violently pulling on the doorknob. It flies off in his hand, hurling him across the room. He smashes into the opposite wall and slides to the floor.

He picks himself up and crosses back to the locked door. He runs his hand across the surface of it. It's hard wood and feels like it could be over two inches thick.

He looks around the room for something to hit it with.

CUT TO

INT. THE OPERA STAGE – NIGHT.

SCARPIA is giving orders to SPOLETTA, one of his men.

>   SPOLETTA
>   *(singing)*
> A firing squad.

>   SCARPIA
>   *(singing quickly, with marked meaning)*
> A sham one! As in the case of Palmieri! Is
> it properly understood?

>   SPOLETTA
>   *(singing)*
> I fully understand.

>   SCARPIA
>   *(singing)*
> Go.

Panning off SCARPIA into the wings.

BASSENE is into the full emotion of the opera. He mimes along with singers acting out the opera with them.

Panning off BASSENE to CHRISTE and VIDEO CREW.

JUAN is shooting some great stuff but CHRISTE is going crazy with tension. She's using all of her self-control to keep from running out of the theatre and joining the search for RUBEN.

Behind her are a group of SKULL-MASKED SOLDIERS. One of them, PRINCE CHARMING, drifts up behind her.

He slips something in her hand as he whispers in her ear.

CHRISTE's head jerks.

She's been kissed.

The opera is so loud at this point that we can't hear what PRINCE CHARMING is saying to her.

CHRISTE's heads jerks again.

PRINCE CHARMING moves back away from her and disappears into a GROUP OF SOLDIERS.

INT. DOWNSTAIRS FOYER – NIGHT.

WOLFE smashes the door with the claw end of a hammer. It digs into the wood.

With both hands, he pulls the hammer out. A large chunk of wood falls to the floor. He smashes the claw back into the hole. It digs deeper into the shattered wood. He pulls the hammer out again. Another large chunk of the door falls to the floor.

He pulls the hammer back and with all his strength lets it fly.

INT. OPERA STAGE – NIGHT.

While SCARPIA is writing, TOSCA approaches the table and with a trembling hand takes a glass of wine. As she raises it to her lips she sees on the table a sharp-pointed knife. She casts a quick glance at SCARPIA who at that moment is busy writing, and, with infinite caution, she picks up the knife.

She hides it behind her, leaning on the table and watching SCARPIA finish writing. He stands up, folds the paper, and opening his arms, advances on TOSCA to embrace her.

                    SCARPIA
                    (*singing*)
              Tosca, at last you are mine!

His tone of rapture changes to a terrible cry: TOSCA has stabbed him in the heart.

                     TOSCA
                    (*singing*)
               That was Tosca's kiss!

SCARPIA, staggering, tries to clutch at TOSCA, who recoils in terror.

                    SCARPIA
                    (*singing*)
                 Help! I'm dying.

Panning off the dying CARPIA to BASSENE in the wings.

He is acting out SCARPIA's death dance.

Continue passing to JOSE shooting BASSENE and then over to CHRISTE.

Her face is calm. Emotionless.

Continue panning down CHRISTE's arm to her hand.

She holds a gun.

INT. DOWNSTAIRS FOYER – NIGHT.

WOLFE smashes the claw through the door. The hole is big enough for him to stick his hand through it.

He turns the lock from the other side. The door swings open.

He pulls his hand out of the hole and runs down the cellar steps.

Panning from the open door to the living room window.

There on the porch is an APPREHENSIVE NEIGHBOR. She is in her sixties but her hearing is still good. She yells to her DAUGHTER behind her.

                    NEIGHBOR
          Call the police!

INT. CELLAR – NIGHT.

It's pitch dark.

WOLFE takes out a lighter and flicks it.

The tiny flame illuminates the room. Lying at his feet are the bodies of RUBEN and MIGUEL.

He kneels down and checks their vital signs.

SERRANO'S dead, but the boy is alive.

WOLFE shakes RUBEN and his eyes slowly open.

                    WOLFE
          Are you all right?

                    RUBEN
          So sleepy.

INT. FOYER – NIGHT.

WOLFE comes out of the cellar carrying RUBEN in his arms. He goes out the front door.

EXT. PORCH – NIGHT.

WOLFE comes out on the porch to face the NEIGHBOR. She fearfully backs away from him.

                    NEIGHBOR
            Don't try anything Mister. My daughter
            called the police.

                     WOLFE
            Good. Where's your phone? I want to call
            an ambulance.

INT. OPERA STAGE – NIGHT.

It's act three. The set is the Platform of the Castel Sant' Angelo. To the left, a casement, furnished with a table, a bench, and a stool. To the right is a small staircase leading up to the platform that extends out over the orchestra pit. In the background is the Vatican and St. Peter's. The sky is that uncertain grey that proceeds the dawn.

CAVARADOSSI sits at the desk and writes a note.

                  CAVARADOSSI
                    (*singing*)
            And the stars were shining. The earth
            smelt sweet. The garden gate creaked.
            And a footstep brushed the sand. She
            entered, fragrant, and fell into my arms.

Panning off CAVARADOSSI to the wings.

BASSENE is sobbing. JUAN is getting it all on video. Next to the CAMERA CREW stands CHRISTE. Still emotionless. Waiting.

Panning down her arm we pass the gun and settle on her handbag. It rests on her hip.

We move into CHRISTE's bag and start to hear something under the very loud singing of CAVARADOSSI.

It's the faint ringing of CHRISTE's cellular phone.

INT. NEIGHBORS' HOUSE – NIGHT.

WOLFE grips the phone in frustration.

Across the room he looks at RUBEN asleep in a chair. The NEIGHBOR sits on the arm of the chair gently stroking the boy's hair with motherly concern.

>   WOLFE
> Damn! Why isn't she answering?

Finally at the tenth ring, WOLFE hears a click and singing from the opera stage.

>   WOLFE
> Christe! Thank God! Look I found
> Ruben. He was drugged but he's fine.
> I called an ambulance and it's on the way.
>   (*there is no response*)
> Christe are you there?

>   CHRISTE
>   (*over the phone, emotionless*)
> Yes.

>   WOLFE
> I found Ruben!

>   CHRISTE
>   (*emotionless*)
> Yes.

>   WOLFE
>   (*suspicious*)
> Christe. Are you all right?

>   CHRISTE
> Yes.

                    WOLFE
　What are you doing?

                    CHRISTE
　Waiting.

                    WOLFE
　Waiting for what?

                    CHRISTE
　The firing squad to shoot.

                    WOLFE
　Then what are you going to do?

                    CHRISTE
　Shoot the president.

                    WOLFE
　Oh my God.
              (*thinking for second,
              then loud and commanding*)
　Ambrose Chapel!

                                              CUT TO

INT. WINGS – NIGHT.

CHRISTE, holding her phone to her ear, jerks.

                                              CUT TO

Opera glass binocular shot of CHRISTE.

                                              CUT TO

The face of the MAN holding the opera glasses.

He looks familiar but the opera glasses obscure his face.

We pull away to see he's filling the once-vacant seat next to KEEN.

CUT TO

INT. NEIGHBORS' HOUSE – NIGHT.

WOLFE on the phone.

> WOLFE
> (*loud and firm*)
> DO NOTHING BUT ANSWER THIS PHONE.

INT. WINGS – NIGHT.

CHRISTE jerks again.
She pushes the "end" button on her phone, disconnecting.

INT. NEIGHBORS' HOUSE – NIGHT.

WOLFE listens to a dead line.

He drops the phone and races out of the door.

INT. STAGE – NIGHT.

TOSCA and CAVARADOSSI are in an embrace. From the small staircase a squad of soldiers wearing skull masks follows an OFFICER up onto the platform.

SPOLETTA, the SERGEANT and the JAILOR come behind them. SPOLETTA gives the necessary instructions. The sky brightens: it is dawn. A bell strikes four o'clock.

The JAILER approaches CAVARADOSSI, and, taking off his hat, motions the OFFICER.

> JAILER
> (*singing*)
> It's time!

                    CAVARADOSSI
                     (*singing*)
I'm ready.

                       TOSCA
           (*singing in a very low voice to
            Cavaradossi, concealing a laugh*)
          Now remember: at the first shot, down!

                    CAVARADOSSI
                     (*singing*)
Down.

                       TOSCA
                     (*singing*)
            And don't get up before I call you.

                    CAVARADOSSI
                     (*singing*)
No, love.

                                                CUT TO

INT. WINGS – NIGHT.

CHRISTE, motionless, holding the gun in one hand, the phone in the other.

She waits for the next call.

                                                CUT TO

MAJOR BACON'S BOX.

MAJOR, SPECTOR, KEEN and the again vacant seat next to them.

KEEN is looking through the opera glasses.

CUT TO

KEEN's POV through the opera glasses.

He is studying the group of soldiers looking for PRINCE CHARMING. He can't tell which one he is because they all wear skull masks.

KEEN pans the glasses over to the presidential box.

The PRESIDENT leans forward, caught up in the emotion of the opera.

                    SPECTOR
                    (*to Keen*)
Who changed her instructions?

                    KEEN
I don't know. But it's being taken care of.

                    MAJOR
Shhhhh! Could you take the conversation somewhere else!

EXT. PALACIO DE BELLAS ARTES (MEXICAN CITY OPERA HOUSE) – NIGHT.

WOLFE jumps out of a cab and runs up the steps of the opera house.

INT. LOBBY – NIGHT.

WOLFE races through the lobby, heading for the center aisle entrance.

An USHER blocks his path.

                    USHER
Excuse me, sir.

WOLFE
What?

USHER
Could I see your ticket?

WOLFE
I don't have a ticket. I'm with Christe Rivera. Channel One.

USHER
Do you have a press pass?

WOLFE
(*urgent*)
No I don't have a press pass. Look! You have to let me in!

USHER
Do you know where Mrs. Rivera is?

WOLFE
Backstage somewhere. I can't stand here and talk to you.

USHER
(*motioning to two security men across the lobby*)
Why don't you just wait here until the opera's over. It will just be a few minutes. Then I'm sure…

WOLFE tries to push past him but the TWO SECURITY GUARDS grab him from behind.

There's a brief struggle ending with WOLFE being pinned to the ground.

Suddenly he hears a familiar voice.

MONTANA
What are you men doing? That's Dr.
Nicholas Wolfe!

MONTANA pulls the SECURITY GUARDS off WOLFE.

MONTANA
Don't you realize who this man is?

SECURITY GUARD
Somebody trying to force his way into
the theatre?

MONTANA
Don't be ridiculous. This man is a world-
renowned psychiatrist. He won the Nobel
Prize last year.

SECURITY GUARD
Well, he's sure not acting like any Nobel
Prize winner.

MONTANA
(*helping Nick to his feet*)
C'mon Nick, let me get you some water.

DR. MONTANA throws WOLFE's ARM over his shoulder and helps him walk over to a flight of stairs at the far left of the lobby.

The SECURITY GUARDS shake their heads as they watch them go.

WOLFE
(*smiling*)
Nobel Prize, huh?

MONTANA
(*chuckling*)
I had to tell them something to stop them from killing you.

WOLFE
Thank God you did. I've got to find Christe.

MONTANA
What happened?

WOLFE
(*breathless*)
She got her instructions to kill the president.

MONTANA
How do you know?

WOLFE
I talked to her on the phone.

MONTANA
Christ! We've got to stop her.

WOLFE
I did, I think. On the phone. I said the password and told her to do nothing until I called her again.

MONTANA
Are you sure it worked?

WOLFE
How do I know? I've never programmed anybody.

At the end of the lobby, they reach the top of a long downward flight of stairs.

MONTANA
Be careful. These stairs are marble.

DR. MONTANA slips his other arm around WOLFE's waist. They slowly move down the stairs.

WOLFE
(*trying to turn to go back up*)
But I've got to get to her.

MONTANA
She's waiting to be called, isn't she? There are some phones downstairs.
(*he looks up to listen to the opera*)
Hear that? We're missing the best part.

WOLFE looks up.

Suddenly MONTANA gives WOLFE a brutal shove propelling him down the hard stone staircase.

WOLFE tumbles violently down thirty bone-bruising steps, crashing to floor in a twisted heap.

MONTANA rushes down the stairs, past the barely conscious WOLFE, and into a phone booth.

He quickly dials a number.

CUT TO

CHRISTE's bag.

The cellular phone rings.

She reaches in for it and puts it to her ear.

MONTANA
(*on the phone*)
Ambrose Chapel!

CHRISTE's head jerks.

> MONTANA
> (*on the phone*)
> After the firing squad shoots, shoot your
> father. Then aim the gun into the audience
> and continue firing.

CHRISTE's head jerks again.

She drops the phone back into her bag and looks up to the stage.

INT. STAGE – NIGHT.

The SERGEANT leads CAVARADOSSI to the apron of the stage. He turns him around so his back faces the audience. The SERGEANT goes to blindfold him but CAVARADOSSI smilingly refuses.

TOSCA is on the left of the casement, upstage center. She stands on a slightly raised platform so that she can see her lover clearly.

> TOSCA
> (*singing*)
> How long this delay is! What are they still
> waiting for? The sun's up already. I know
> it's only play acting but the suspense
> seems endless!

CUT TO

INT. DOWNSTAIRS LOBBY – NIGHT.

MONTANA grips WOLFE by his hair. He savagely pulls WOLFE's head close to his.

                    MONTANA
          You almost fucked up everything.
          But I just gave Sleeping Beauty new
          improved instructions. She's now our Jack
          Ruby. Wreaking mad vengeance on the
          president's murderer. And you had a part
          to play too: The professional witness to
          Christe's tragic psychotic breakdown.

                                           CUT TO

INT. THE STAGE.

The OFFICER and SERGEANT lead the FIRING SQUAD to their position. They line up, downstage center, facing CAVARADOSSI.

                                           CUT TO

INT. DOWNSTAIRS LOBBY – NIGHT.

                    WOLFE
                (barely conscious)
          How did you?

                    MONTANA
          Keen used Bacon's money to finance my
          mind control research. We put the plan
          into operation when Christe's father was
          a double agent in Beirut. The perfect place
          to program her, because if the plot was
          ever discovered? It could only be traced
          back to Shiite terrorists.

CUT TO

INT. STAGE – NIGHT.

> MONTANA
> (*voiceover*)
> Then? We waited for '96. Keen knew Major couldn't beat the president in a general election, but with the right dramatic circumstances, like what is going to happen in the next few minutes, he knew Major would be swept into office in a huge public outburst of emotion.

The FIRING SQUAD load their rifles.

THE LAST SOLDIER on the left turns toward CHRISTE. He stares at her for a moment.

CHRISTE looks up into his eyes. She recognizes her FATHER.

He smiles at her. She stares back, emotionless. He is nothing but a target to her. She grips the gun in her hand.

PRINCE CHARMING turns away and mimes loading his rifle.

CUT TO

INT. DOWNSTAIRS LOBBY – NIGHT.

> MONTANA
> I've read Keen's speech. It's historic. Too bad you're not going to be around to hear it. But you had such a terrible fall.
> (*grabs hold of Nick's head with his other hand*)
> It snapped your neck.

He grips WOLFE's head and gives it a violent counter-clockwise wrench.

Anticipating this move, WOLFE rolls with the counter-clockwise motion and instead of MONTANA breaking his neck, WOLFE rolls over on top of him.

WOLFE immediately grabs MONTANA by the hair and bashes his head into the marble floor.

MONTANA lies there, still.

WOLFE pulls himself to his feet. His whole body racked with pain. He slowly turns toward the steps and starts back up.

CUT TO

The firing squad slowing raising their rifles.

CUT TO

THE PRESIDENT'S BOX.

THE SECRET SERVICE MEN, seeing the rifles pointed in the PRESIDENT's direction from the stage, immediately jump up to shield him.

The PRESIDENT, smiling, motions them to sit down.

CUT TO

MAJOR BACON'S BOX.

KEEN has his binoculars pointed at CHRISTE. She starts to raise her pistol.

CUT TO

CHRISTE raising her pistol, aiming it at her FATHER.

CUT TO

CHRISTE'S POV OF HER FATHER.

PRINCE CHARMING aims his rifle.

CUT TO

PRINCE CHARMING's POV of the PRESIDENT.

PRINCE CHARMING aims his rifle over CAVARA-DOSSI'S HEAD and at the PRESIDENT.

CUT TO

TOSCA, who puts her hands to her ears.

CUT TO

The OFFICER, starting to lower his saber.

CUT TO

Center aisle doors. WOLFE bursts through the door. He madly runs down the center aisle chased by the security guards. He looks up at the firing squad on the platform.

CUT TO

WOLFE's POV of the firing squad about to fire.

CUT TO

WOLFE's face. A look of horror.

Then he looks up at the PRESIDENT.

CUT TO

WOLFE's POV of the PRESIDENT, who is leaning forward in his box, totally caught up in the drama of the opera.

CUT TO

WOLFE looks back to the stage.

CUT TO

The OFFICER lowering his saber.

CUT TO

Zoom into WOLFE's face.

CUT TO

WOLFE's POV. Zoom into PRINCE CHARMING at the end

CUT TO

CLOSE SHOT: WOLFE's face.

He screams.

              WOLFE
NO!

The firing squad fires.

CAVARADOSSI falls to the floor.

CUT TO

The PRESIDENT leaping to his feet.

His shoulder is suddenly bloody. He avoided the head shot because of his sudden move. Still, his head is completely exposed.

CUT TO

PRINCE CHARMING now lining up a fatal head shot. He starts to pull the trigger again.

Suddenly a bullet rips through his side.

PRINCE CHARMING falls to the floor.
He turns toward the shooter.

CUT TO

CHRISTE, now onstage, holds a smoking gun.
Her face is expressionless.

CUT TO

MAJOR and KEEN standing up.

They watch the PRESIDENT disappear behind a wall of bodies.

> MAJOR
> What the hell is going on?

CUT TO

CHRISTE. She slowly turns the gun on the panicked audience.

CUT TO

PRINCE CHARMING on the floor of the stage.
He looks over at his betrayers.

CUT TO

PRINCE CHARMING's POV of MAJOR and KEEN.

CUT TO

PRINCE CHARMING painfully raises his rifle.

CUT TO

CHRISTE, who watches WOLFE racing down the aisle toward her. She aims the gun at him.

CUT TO

WOLFE running toward the stage, watching CHRISTE in horror.

CUT TO

THE PRESIDENT's box.

A SECRET SERVICE MAN sees CHRISTE's raised gun.

CUT TO

PRINCE CHARMING fires two shots.

CUT TO

SPECTOR and KEEN falling.

They are both hit in the heart.

MAJOR dives for cover.

CUT TO

THE SECRET SERVICE MAN aiming at CHRISTE.

CUT TO

CHRISTE. She slowly squeezes the trigger.

CUT TO

WOLFE. He jumps on the stage.

CUT TO

THE SECRET SERVICE MAN's clean shot is blocked by WOLFE.

CUT TO

WOLFE running toward CHRISTE, her gun aimed right in his face.

CUT TO

WOLFE screaming.

> WOLFE
> AMBROSE CHAPEL!

CUT TO

CHRISTE. Her head jerks.

CUT TO

WOLFE, slowing up, now just a few feet away.

> WOLFE
> COME TO ME!

CUT TO

CHRISTE, her head jerks again and she drops the gun and walks over to WOLFE.

WOLFE pulls CHRISTE into his arms protecting her from the arsenal of guns now aimed at her from the president's box.

> CHRISTE
> (*waking out of the trance*)
> What happened?

CUT TO

The Man Who Knew Too Much. The cymbals clash together.

JO (DORIS DAY) leaps forward with a scream.

The DIGNITARY clutches his arm and slumps forward.

The people around JO, startled, as they rise in their seat and turn back to her.

BEN (JIMMY STEWART) dashes into the ASSASSIN's box.

The ASSASSIN turns toward him, pulling his gun.

BEN lunges forward with a blow.

The ASSASSIN staggers back and we hear the clatter of the gun as it falls to the floor.

He immediately turns toward the camera looking for a means of escape. He leaps to the edge of the box to go over to the next one. He slips.

We see the ASSASSIN fall with a crash into the aisle.

Pull back to reveal: this scene is being projected on a movie screen.

Panning off the screen, we discover we're in a nearly deserted movie theatre.

We move into a COUPLE passionately necking in the tenth row.

It's CHRISTE and WOLFE.

CHRISTE pulls away, takes a brief look at the screen. In that look we see that all of this is behind her.

CHRISTE leans in, and smiling, whispers in WOLFE's ear.

                    CHRISTE
    Drowning yet?

Fade to black.

THE END.

www.ingramcontent.com/pod-product-compliance
Lightning Source LLC
Chambersburg PA
CBHW070142080526
44586CB00015B/1797